Early Praise for *Build a Binary Clock with Elixir and Nerves*

It's tough to write a book that a beginner and an expert can both enjoy. Frank and Bruce do an excellent job of walking through what it takes to build a real, working embedded software project and how simple it is with Elixir and Nerves.

➤ **Mike Waud**
   Senior Software Engineer, SparkMeter

This book is a great resource for onboarding a non-embedded programmer to the embedded device development using Elixir and Nerves. When I first started Nerves as an embedded device beginner, it was quite challenging to understand all the hardware-related terminology and concepts. With this book in hand, one will be able to learn all the basics step by step with little frustration. It teaches not only the embedded development itself but also useful techniques for organizing code so our programs can be easy to maintain.

➤ **Masatoshi Nishiguchi**
   Software Engineer

Bruce and Frank's exciting journey to build a binary clock illustrates highly effective design patterns that are especially well suited for Nerves and the tremendous potential LiveBook brings to Nerves for engineering creativity amidst a global chip shortage.

➤ **Jason Johnson**
   Worker-Owner, FullSteam Labs

Build a Binary Clock
with Elixir and Nerves

Use Layering to Produce Better Embedded Systems

Frank Hunleth

Bruce A. Tate

The Pragmatic Bookshelf

Raleigh, North Carolina

Many of the designations used by manufacturers and sellers to distinguish their products are claimed as trademarks. Where those designations appear in this book, and The Pragmatic Programmers, LLC was aware of a trademark claim, the designations have been printed in initial capital letters or in all capitals. The Pragmatic Starter Kit, The Pragmatic Programmer, Pragmatic Programming, Pragmatic Bookshelf, PragProg and the linking *g* device are trademarks of The Pragmatic Programmers, LLC.

Every precaution was taken in the preparation of this book. However, the publisher assumes no responsibility for errors or omissions, or for damages that may result from the use of information (including program listings) contained herein.

For our complete catalog of hands-on, practical, and Pragmatic content for software developers, please visit *https://pragprog.com*.

The team that produced this book includes:

CEO: Dave Rankin
COO: Janet Furlow
Managing Editor: Tammy Coron
Development Editor: Jacquelyn Carter
Copy Editor: L. Sakhi MacMillan
Layout: Gilson Graphics
Founders: Andy Hunt and Dave Thomas

For sales, volume licensing, and support, please contact *support@pragprog.com*.

For international rights, please contact *rights@pragprog.com*.

ISBN-13: 978-1-68050-923-6
Book version: P1.0—August 2022

Contents

Acknowledgments

Though this cover prominently highlights two authors like a couple of shining LEDs, the real story behind the story is one of a much greater team. In these short paragraphs, we'll try to thank those who made this book possible.

First, we'd like to thank the wonderful staff at The Pragmatic Bookshelf for all of their help and support. The staff has always provided unwavering support to Elixir. We offer special thanks to our friend and editor Jackie Carter who tirelessly works to get more out of us. She's our friend and our ally. Thanks for being there.

José Valim, you have created something lasting and remarkable. Your creation of Elixir and stewardship of the community has had an incalculable impact on all of our careers, and we are all profoundly grateful for what you do to continue to push the language, ecosystem, and infrastructure forward. Your insightful leadership with LiveBook had a direct impact on this book.

We also thank Jonatan Kłosko for your creation of LiveBook. It gave us a story to tell even when supply problems were crushing the rest of this book.

Of course, we thank our reviewers Denver Smith, Kim Shrier, Masatoshi Nishiguchi, Mike Waud, and Jason Johnson. Reviewing a book with hardware has an extra level of commitment that most books don't. Thanks for building out the project and being patient with the words that were sometimes too expert or too basic. You helped form a bridge between this team of authors.

Thanks go also to the Nerves Core Team of Jon Carstens, Connor Rigby, and Masatoshi Nishiguchi. They have shown incredible flexibility and judgement. Nerves wouldn't be possible without a dependable core group of maintainers.

Next, we thank the Nerves community. Thanks for being a welcoming and fun place to hang out and experiment with hardware using Elixir.

Finally, we thank the Elixir community and our readers. Authors write to share. Without someone to read what we have to say, the words are empty.

Frank Hunleth

Writing takes time and focus, especially in this time of pandemic and shortage. I would like to personally thank my wife and two daughters for their love and support. All of you bring so much joy to my life, and I can't imagine how I would have gotten through the stress of finding ways to work around hardware shortages that affected this book without you. Thanks also to Jonatan Kłosko for writing LiveBook and your remarkable customer service as I worked on Nerves LiveBook. The process was way smoother than it had a right to be.

Bruce, thanks for initiating this amazing journey. I can't wait to see where it takes us.

Bruce Tate

Writing is one of my great joys, but it sometimes takes away from family time. I would like to thank my wife and daughters for their support and understanding. Maggie, thanks for all of your love and support through fifteen books and counting. I love you. Julia and Kayla, I am amazed at what you are becoming. I love you both.

Frank, thanks for your extra measure of support as I took on this project while traveling the Great Loop. Alexa and Frank, your visit on our loop with a wonderful gift inspired and energized me.

Introduction

This book is one of a series of books about Elixir and Nerves. Each book in this series will teach one fundamental software concept and build one complete project using the Elixir language on Nerves. Elixir[1] is a highly concurrent and reliable functional programming language, and Nerves[2] is a tool for embedding programs on it to build the internet of things, IoT. These devices are small special-purpose computers used to control hardware. They show up in cars, appliances, and more. You might see these nifty devices called different names. In this book, we'll use the terms target, embedded computer, embedded device, controller, and more depending on the context. Regardless of the name, the concepts are the same. We embed a sophisticated program into a tiny computer.

In this book, you'll build such an IoT device—a *binary clock* that cryptically tells time by lighting a series of LEDs and gets the current time from the network. Pure Elixir code will control the clock's display. While a clock is a relatively simple machine, it has many of the same parts as real-life hardware projects. Throughout this book, you'll use the very same principles to organize the software in your own clock as you'd use in any other program.

How to Read This Book

This book takes you step by step through the process of building an end-to-end binary clock, from the layers of software to the LEDs. If you choose to omit steps, you could wind up with a nonfunctional end product.

Who This Book Is For

This book is for any Elixir programmer who is comfortable with the basics of the programming language and is interested in dabbling in the world of

---

1.   https://elixir-lang.org
2.   http://nerves-project.org/

embedded systems. No soldering or deep hardware experience is necessary, given that you will be working with off-the-shelf plugin-and-play hardware.

Who This Book Isn't For

If you have just a little experience with Elixir, don't worry. We'll help you with some of the more advanced concepts. If you are just getting started, you might want to put this book aside for a bit and pick up *Programming Elixir 1.6* *[Tho18]*.

While Elixir 1.6 came out a few years ago now, the core language has not changed much in that time and as such the book will help you develop a solid Elixir foundation. After you read that book, feel free to pick this one up again and get your hands dirty with an IoT-based project.

Building the Project

Being able to build and run your application code will be key to understanding the concepts outlined in this book. As such it is important that you have the items outlined in the next couple sections so that you have everything you need to complete the binary clock.

Software Requirements

Embedded hardware aside, you'll need the following things:

- Elixir version 1.12 or greater
- A Linux, MacOS, or Windows machine to do your development on
- A wireless access point for your local area network

If you have all of those items, then you're good to go from a development machine perspective, and all that is needed is the Nerves related hardware.

Hardware Requirements

While there is some flexibility with what hardware (like what version Raspberry Pi) you can buy and from where, the following items were used by the authors:

- Raspberry Pi Zero W with headers
- Micro-USB connection data cables
- 4GB+ microSD card
- MicroSD card reader
- 20 LEDs of various colors
- Some resistors
- TLC5947 constant current driver with a SPI interface
- Jumper wires, breadboard, headers, and ribbon cables

If you don't know what these things are or where to buy them, fear not, as we explain all of this in the first few chapters. You can drift away from these parts, but you might need to change the instructions in the book slightly to get things to run.

Online Resources

All of the code for this project can be found online in the GitHub repository.[3] If you need any assistance for all things Elixir and Nerves, be sure to check out the Elixir Forums[4] where you'll find a vibrant community ready to help. Make sure you mark your post with the Nerves category so the Nerves team will see your post.

If instead you would rather use a more interactive feedback system, the #nerves channel on the Elixir Slack may be your best bet. Since this forum maintains history, the Nerves team prefers this resource so their advice can help many users with the same concerns. If you choose to use Slack, consider adding a post to Elixir Forum to document your problem resolution.

With those bits of housekeeping aside, we can make a plan.

---

3. https://github.com/groxio-learning/thnerves
4. https://elixirforum.com

Part I

The Prototype

Hardware development works best in small increments. In the first few chapters, we'll take some short, sure steps toward a working clock. The first stride is a simple, working Nerves project so we can build and deploy custom software into custom hardware. The initial system won't be much, just a few lines of software and a circuit that blinks an LED. It doesn't seem like much, but this initial project will serve as a foundation we can morph into the final project, one tiny step at a time.

CHAPTER 1

Our Plan

It's often hard to get started when working with hardware because there are so many small things that can go wrong. For that reason, it's important to establish several small, quick wins instead of making one full project work end to end. So it is with Nerves.

We're going to direct you to the excellent Nerves documentation to get started. Then we'll shift toward building a networked project that will eventually control our clock. Here's what the plan looks like in detail.

Burn Firmware

Nerves works by combining the Elixir programs that you write with everything else that a specialized embedded device needs to run. An increasing number of these tiny devices actually run the Unix operating system, and Nerves is built to run on them.

You'll start by installing a firmware program written by the Nerves team on an embedded computer, called a *target*. This first step will verify that you can use your Nerves tool chain to install a program on the target's firmware chip. Then you'll snap the firmware chip into your target and connect to it using a USB cable so you can remotely access an Elixir shell. When you're done, you'll know:

- You have a working Nerves tool chain for burning firmware.
- You can use your host to debug your target.

With working firmware, we can shift to the hardware.

Make a Circuit

The first step in building a complex hardware project is to build a simple one that works. It makes sense, then, to build the simplest of circuits, a single

LED that you'll control with your target. Once you've done that much, you'll connect to your target from your development computer, called a *host*, to control the LED. This step will demonstrate that you can build circuits, install them on a target, and control them with a host. When you're done, you'll know:

- You have a working circuit.
- You can exercise your circuit using IEx to talk to programs on firmware.

With a working firmware process and a circuit, the next step is to write a simple program.

Build a Program in Layers

After burning an existing project onto firmware, you'll write your own mix project. You'll add *compilation for a target* to your tool chain. Nerves will build an image that has your program and everything else your embedded device needs.

After you've built a program to blink an LED, you'll build in networking so you can push software changes and share data with the outside world. We'll track a common time. When you're done, you'll know how to:

- Write your own programs, and then burn them onto firmware.

- Build software in layers, with functional cores that handle logic and boundaries to handle external interfaces.

- Connect to your embedded device from networked computers to burn firmware, collect data, or use circuits you build, like your LED circuit.

When this step is done, you'll have a working Nerves skeleton. Your *host* will have proven tools to upload firmware. Your *target* will have a working *circuit*. Finally, your *program* will control the *target*. Those three tiny steps will reap huge rewards in your confidence in a working system and demonstrate any problems before you have to move on.

 Bruce says:
Write Your Software in Layers

The trick to handling complexity is not eliminating it but figuring out ways to deal with a little bit at a time. That's why you should write your programs in layers. Your project will be complex, but the module in your editor window doesn't have to be.

After we've established working firmware uploads, hardware, and software, we can move on to the next part of the book, building the clock. We'll save that plan for later.

Every future Nerves step will have these steps. You'll build circuits, write or update layered programs, and then push them to your firmware.

That's enough planning. We're ready to build a clock.

CHAPTER 2

Burn Firmware

In this book, you'll build a binary clock in two parts. The *circuit* will have individual LEDs that represent a binary clock. The *controller* will have working software to control the clock. In this chapter, we'll pick a target controller and set up working *firmware* we'll use to control the circuit. In later chapters, we'll enhance the circuit and software step by step until we have a working clock.

This first part of the project can be devastatingly complex if you don't know how Nerves works, but by taking one step at a time, you can limit potential problems.

 Frank says:
Take One Small Step at a Time

When you're developing a system with both hardware and software, there are many small decisions to make. I tell both beginners and experts to take one small step at a time. Building Nerves projects in this way simplifies your debugging when you make a mistake.

Let's get started.

This project involves purchasing a target and loading a working Nerves program. Then you'll talk to the target from your host. You'll want to make one tiny step at a time, so in this initial project, you won't write your own program. Instead, you'll load up a known working piece of firmware onto your target.

Here's how we'll proceed. This list of tasks will get you to the point where you've loaded firmware and confirmed that your computer is working:

- Choose a target computer.
- Get all of the hardware you'll need.
- Install a tool to load your firmware.
- Download and burn firmware for your target.
- Connect to your host computer and explore it in IEx.
- Establish a network connection.

That's a long list, but aside from the shopping trip, the project is going to go quickly. Before you can install a firmware, you need a target and a few simple tools. Let's pick a computer.

Choose a Computer

For this initial project, your target will need to be able to do at least two things.

First, it must be on one of the two Nerves target lists. The first list of officially supported hardware[1] contains the list of targets that the Nerves team will help support, but if a computer you want to use isn't there, you can check the second list of community-supported hardware[2] for a more exhaustive list. Unless you're experienced with Nerves, stay with computers on the first list.

The second requirement is connectivity. You need a computer with wireless networking and a USB connection port so the clock will start with the correct time.

Luckily, in recent years a new wave of tiny general-purpose computers have entered production. These computers are small, cheap, and powerful. Among the most popular ones for makers is the Raspberry Pi. One version of that computer, the Raspberry Pi Zero W, is *usually* available for around twelve bucks and is shown in the figure on page 9.

You probably noticed we said "usually available." From 2020 to 2022, supply problems have crippled electronics markets, and Raspberry Pis are not immune. If you can't find a new Raspberry Pi from traditional sources, you might try alternative means. One such source is the Raspberry Pi locator.[3] If you have to wait for supplies, all is not lost. Many of the projects in this book run on traditional desktops and in tests. You can read through a chapter and run your projects on your desktop until you get your Raspberry Pi.

Slightly larger than a pack of gum, the Pi Zero has onboard wireless and bluetooth, and you can see in the figure the two micro-USB ports on the right

---

1. https://hexdocs.pm/nerves/targets.html
2. https://hex.pm/packages?search=depends:nerves_system_br
3. https://rpilocator.com/

side near the top and an onboard microSD card on the bottom with a loaded card. On the left, you can see pins for interaction. We'll initially use them to flash an LED, and later we'll use them to control a bunch of LEDs through a common interface.

Frank says:
Why the Raspberry Pi Zero W?

The Raspberry Pi Zero W is small, inexpensive, and plenty fast for running many Nerves programs. Plus you only need one USB cable to get started working with it. This combination of performance, features, and price is hard to beat for an embedded computer.

Now that you know your target embedded system, you can build a shopping list.

Project Shopping List

Our shopping list is divided into three parts. The first one will get you through the firmware project. The second list, in the next chapter, will deal with the LEDs. The final list in the last chapter will point you to a custom-printed circuit board for those who have trouble getting parts or who might want a more integrated experience.

This first shopping list specifies a target computer with *headers* pre-soldered on so you can connect your own wires to the various pins. You also need a microSD card and a reader to go with it. Finally, you'll need a micro-USB cable that will work with whatever USB connections your personal computer supports.

- Raspberry Pi Zero with headers[4]

- MicroSD card[5]

- MicroSD card reader (depends on your computer)

- Micro-USB to USB (depends on your computer; the micro-USB is for the Raspberry Pi, and you'll need to connect it to a USB connection your computer supports)

- If you want to shop for both projects in this chapter, add the contents of The Shopping List, on page 15

We've included links from a builder community called AdaFruit because they have decent prices and excellent support for makers. We couldn't pick a USB cable or reader for you because the product will vary based on the interface your computer supports. Remember, you might not be able to find Raspberry Pis from traditional sources. If not, check out the rpilocator website[6] for some options.

USB Power and Data Cables Are Different

 Take note. USB cables for data and power function differently. You can use data cables for power, but you can't transfer data over power cables! This problem has tripped up experts and novices alike.

While you're at it, if you don't have a piece of breadboard and a few LEDs and resistors laying around, you might scan ahead and get those parts too, using the link at the end of the previous list. Overall, you can probably get everything on the list pretty inexpensively, especially if you already have wires, cards, and readers around.

---

4.   https://www.adafruit.com/product/3708
5.   https://www.adafruit.com/product/2693
6.   https://rpilocator.com/

Install Nerves

If you haven't already done so, you'll need to install or update Nerves.[7] It has tools to compile Elixir, assemble the operating system software needed for a host, burn firmware, debug, and manage projects. To make use of these goodies, you'll need to install Nerves for your environment. Just a quick note about running Nerves on Windows—the Nerves team says:

> If you have issues with any of the tooling after following the steps below, we recommend you reach out to us in the #nerves channel on the Elixir Slack.

If you're having problems with Windows, ensure you've done so.

To use Nerves, you'll need to pick a tool for uploading firmware. This chapter will have directions for fwup and MacOS. To install what you need, follow the directions on the Nerves project install page.[8] When you're done, come back and choose the right target firmware.

Download and Install Firmware

If you're not familiar with Nerves, this quick project will make sure you know how to use Nerves tooling to work with firmware and target computers. Rather than building your own program right off the bat, you're going to download working firmware that's already built. Then you'll install that firmware on your platform, following Quickstart for Elixir Circuits.[9] These instructions roughly follow the instructions on that page. The instructions are similar now, but if you notice some breakage, use the directions in that project instead of this book.

After you've installed fwup or etcher using the QuickStart directions, your next step is to find the firmware for the Raspberry Pi from the Circuits Quickstart firmware list.[10] We chose fwup and the Raspberry Pi Zero, so I will use the circuits_quickstart_rpi0.fw[11] download file. Move the file to a working directory.

When you've done so, plug in your microSD card reader and put a card in it. Just a quick warning—you should be willing to delete whatever is on the card before you copy over the firmware, because you'll lose whatever is on the card.

---

7. https://hexdocs.pm/nerves/updating-projects.html
8. https://hexdocs.pm/nerves/installation.html
9. https://github.com/elixir-circuits/circuits_quickstart
10. https://github.com/elixir-circuits/circuits_quickstart/releases
11. https://github.com/elixir-circuits/circuits_quickstart/releases/download/v0.4.0/circuits_quickstart_rpi0.fw

Card Data Will Be Erased

Take note. The process of burning firmware erases existing microSD card data!

Now, issue the fwup command. If you're really sure fwup can delete the contents of your card, accept the consequences by confirming and authenticating, like this:

```
[burn_test] → fwup circuits_quickstart_rpi0.fw
Use 30.95 GB memory card found at /dev/rdisk6? [y/N] Y
100% [====================================] 32.78 MB in / 35.28 MB out
Success!
Elapsed time: 10.893 s
```

The exact output might change slightly, but if your system is generally making happy messages like Success!, you're good to go. You have working firmware, and you can plug it into your Raspberry Pi Zero. Be sure the copper connectors face down, toward the board, as in the following image:

Believe it or not, your first Nerves project is built. You have a Unix computer that can run Elixir. Let's take it for a test drive!

SSH Through a USB Cable

Now you're going to use the ssh program to remotely shell into the computer using a USB network connection, so connect your Pi Zero to your computer with your micro-USB cable. Remember, data cables and power cables are different beasts![12] The USB cable serves both as a conduit for your networking data and a power source. If all goes well, you'll see the onboard LED flash a couple of times, as shown in the figure on page 13.

---

12. https://github.com/elixir-circuits/circuits_quickstart/issues/101

Using ssh, you'll make a secure connection from your host to target using ssh circuits@nerves.local. The password is circuits:

```
[burn_test] → ssh circuits@nerves.local
SSH server
Enter password for "circuits"
password:   <type:  circuits  >
Interactive Elixir (1.11.1) - press Ctrl+C to exit (type h() ENTER for help)
Toolshed imported. Run h(Toolshed) for more info.

    Elixir Circuits Quickstart
...
```

If all is going well, you'll see the cool ASCII Elixir droplet with a few pointers. Read them and take note. You have a full working IEx console. You can run any commands from the Elixir standard library, like this:

```
iex(2)> [1, 2, 3] |> Enum.reduce(&Kernel.+/2)
6
```

Nice. You can explore the Toolshed goodies and the IEx prompt at your leisure. Now, it's time to build a circuit and put it to use.

What You Built

For your first Nerves project, you used the Circuits QuickStart for a few quick wins. First, you shopped for a few parts for the initial project. Then you burned existing firmware with the Nerves tooling. You connected a Raspberry Pi Zero to your computer through a USB port to establish a remote connection and see what was happening on the board of your target. The Toolshed tools let you rapidly tell what was going on.

That's a lot of work without any custom programming. Still, that step was significant.

Why It Matters

Working with hardware is about establishing quick wins from small steps that are each easy to verify and debug. Uploading firmware establishes the first critical step of a development cycle, building and loading your program.

Similarly, connecting to a computer via an SSH connection over a USB cable seems simple, but it provides the basic set of tools you'll need to verify and debug complex projects.

These tools will come into play as you build Nerves projects with growing complexity. Let's try it out.

Try It Yourself

In this section, you'll explore the Nerves tools that you'll later need to debug projects. The Toolshed API helps you debug your hardware. Here are some *easy* exercises:

- Use Toolshed's cmd to determine the working directory for your Raspberry Pi's IEx session.

- Use Toolshed's top to see which processes are running.

- Start a new Elixir process with spawn and Process.sleep/1. Can you see the new process with top? Why or why not?

- Print a directory tree.

- What is the host name of your Raspberry Pi?

Here is a *medium* exercise.

- Upload the *Nerves LiveBook*[13] to your Raspberry Pi. Solve these exercises using LiveBook. What differences do you notice?

Next Time

In this chapter, we've focused on building a circuit and installing firmware. Next, we'll focus on strategies for building your Nerves projects, layer by layer. When you turn the page, you'll write a basic Nerves project.

---

13. https://github.com/fhunleth/nerves_livebook

CHAPTER 3

Build a Circuit

In the first chapter, we installed known working firmware on a Raspberry Pi. In this chapter, we'll use that firmware to impact the real world. We'll build a circuit. Just as programmers print "Hello, World" as a traditional first program, makers build a blinking LED as a first project.

If you're not yet familiar with electronics, don't worry. We'll help you with the basics. We'll start with a brief introduction to circuits and the techniques makers use to build prototypes. Then we'll plan and build a circuit. When you're done, you'll have a simple circuit you can control with a Nerves program.

Let's get started.

Build an LED Circuit

Our next project will take one step beyond firmware. One of the best things about Nerves is making computers to control real devices in your world. We're going to start by blinking an LED. Since you already know how to shell out to your Raspberry Pi, you'll control an LED from IEx.

To do so, you'll build a circuit and connect it to your Raspberry Pi. Eventually, we'll make a project by soldering components together. For now, since you're just building a temporary project, you'll use a tried-and-true prototyping canvas for circuit building called breadboard.

Let's get started with a second shopping list.

The Shopping List

The previous list had only the Raspberry Pi Zero and a few extra goodies to help you load firmware and connect. You'll need everything you used on that first list, plus the stuff to make your circuit, plus a few wires to connect your circuit to your Raspberry Pi pins. Remember, the final chapter will have an additional printed circuit board for those who want to pursue that additional project. Here's a list of products from the favorite vendor of the Nerves community:

- Everything on Project Shopping List, on page 9 (you only need one of each item on that list)
- 2 packs colored LEDs[1]
- 8 100–500 Ohm resistors[2]
- 4 sets header pins[3]
- 1 breadboard[4]
- 1 set male-to-female jumper wires[5]
- 4 sets female-to-female jumper wires[6]
- 1 set male-to-male jumper wires[7]
- 2 TLC5947 constant current LED drivers[8]

This set will have a few extras, but you'll use them if you play with Nerves for much time, and you may as well take advantage of your shipping costs to throw in a few extra components. Pay attention to the shipping times. There are alternatives for everything on the list if something is sold out. If you're an electronics hobbyist who has worked with circuits on breadboard before, you probably have most if not all of this stuff lying around. If not, you're in for a treat. Order it and when it gets in, you'll be ready to play. There are two constant current drivers on this list because sometimes new hardware developers burn out hardware as they learn to solder.

Let's talk a bit about circuits. If you've not worked with them before, there are a few things you need to know.

---

1. https://www.adafruit.com/product/4203
2. https://www.adafruit.com/product/4293
3. https://www.adafruit.com/product/3002
4. https://www.adafruit.com/product/239
5. https://www.adafruit.com/product/4635
6. https://www.adafruit.com/product/1950
7. https://www.adafruit.com/product/1956
8. https://www.adafruit.com/product/1429

Circuits

Circuits are loops of conductive[9] material. The simplest ones have electricity that flows from a power source[10] and back to the source through a ground.[11]

Components are the functions of the electrical profession. Components transform electricity in various ways. They also sometimes provide side effects such as the production of light or heat. You'll use two components. One is an LED that emits light when you put power through it. The other is a resistor that's only job is to, well, resist. Most circuits need a certain level of resistance to keep its components from overloading.

Here are the various parts of your project and the role the items on the shopping list play.

A conducting loop
   Breadboard

A power source
   One of the Pi's general-purpose IO pins (abbreviated GPIO)

Grounding for the power source
   One of the Pi's ground pins

A light source
   An LED, a component that emits light when power flows through it

A resistor
   A component that resists electricity

We'll look at circuits in a symbolic diagram called a schematic. Here's the schematic for the project:

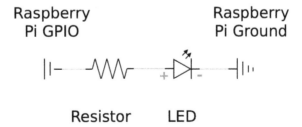

9.   https://www.nde-ed.org/EducationResources/HighSchool/Electricity/conductorsinsulators.htm
10.   https://www.allaboutcircuits.com/textbook/reference/chpt-9/power-sources/
11.   https://en.wikipedia.org/wiki/Ground_(electricity)

The schematic labels each of the components. Notice power flows from the GPIO pin, through the resistor and out, through the positive leg of the LED and out the negative one, and into the ground pin in the Pi.

Let's take a look at how breadboard works.

Breadboard

Breadboard is a reusable block with holes for placing connected components. It's plastic on top, with wires inside, and has spring-loaded sockets that hold components on the bottom. The following image shows a typical piece of breadboard:

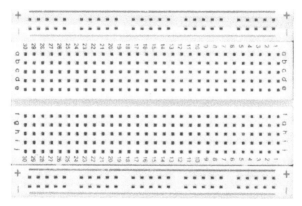

The holes in breadboard have a tension that holds components tight enough to stay in one place, but not so tightly to be permanent. Holes are connected horizontally but disconnected vertically, so you can build circuits of connected components by choosing which holes will hold your components, as shown here:

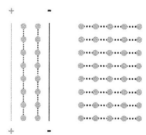

Remember, breadboard's job is to quickly connect components together without soldering or wires. The dots in the diagram represent holes in the breadboard for components or jumper wires. The narrow lines represent internal wiring within the breadboard that connects components together. Some of the wires flow vertically and some flow horizontally. Notice the left-hand side. These dots are connected vertically. If you desire, you can use these connected vertical rails to wire your components to a power source and ground.

Now notice the block of holes to the right. Internal horizontal wires connect them. You can connect two components in a circuit by placing one pin from each one in the same row. In this way, you can connect all of your components together, one by one, to build your temporary circuit.

That description may be confusing and abstract at first, so let's make it more tangible. This is what the LED circuit looks like on breadboard:

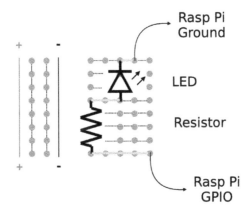

The solid horizontal lines represent the connected wires on the breadboard that make a completed circuit. The black symbols are components. The jagged line is a resistor, and the triangle is your LED. The wide part of the triangle goes to the longer leg, or the positive one. The shorter end is the negative one, and will go to ground. The curved lines represent jumper wires, and will go to the Raspberry Pi. Let's put it together.

Assemble the Circuit

To build your circuit, take an LED and put it on the breadboard, with each leg in a different row. Make note of the longer leg on the LED. That's the positive end—called the annode—and it will go to your power source, the GPIO pin.

Plug one jumper wire on the breadboard, on the same row as the positive end of your LED. Place your resister on the breadboard (you might need to bend the legs down), with one end on the same row as the negative LED terminal and the other end on a new row, the one that will share your last jumper wire. Place your jumper wire next to your resister, and you're done.

Now, it's time to wire up the circuit to the Pi.

Raspberry Pi Pins

Embedded computers get more interesting when they control circuits that interact with real hardware devices. Each of these pins has specific capabilities. Some are power sources that are always on, some are grounds, and some have other purposes. We're interested in the GPIO pins. These pins can be used either to put out power in low or high voltages in output mode or take in power in low or high voltages in input mode.

Our LED circuit makes use of the GPIO pin in output mode. Now it's time to find the GPIO pins using an online tool called pinout.[12] Open it up to see the pin layout of the Pi:

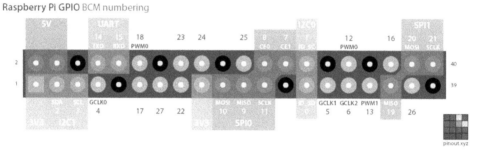

This image is directly from the great folks at Pinout.xyz. As you can imagine, makers that use Raspberry Pis love Pinout.

Remember, your circuit will have power that flows out of your GPIO pin and back into a ground. Let's look at the pinout diagram again. GPIO pins are designated by the green circles in the pinout diagram. We also need a ground, and there are several designated by black circles. We'll use the two pins in the lower right. Each GPIO pin has a number called a Broadcom (BCM) number; note that yours is 26.

Before you do anything else, disconnect your Pi from your computer. We don't want to accidentally cause a short that might damage your new toy. When that's done, you're ready to hook up your hardware.

---

12. https://pinout.xyz

Disconnect Before Wiring

 You should get in the habit of disconnecting your Raspberry Pi from power before you work on your circuits. Otherwise, you might damage or destroy it should you make a mistake.

Connect the jumper cable—the one next to the longer positive leg of your LED—to the power source, your GPIO pin. Then connect the jumper that's next to your resistor to the ground pin. You're now ready to connect power to your Raspberry Pi again.

You have a complete circuit. We'll use an Elixir library to send power to GPIO pin 26. Then power will flow through the jumper, to the LED, to the resistor, and finally back into the Pi ground pin, lighting the LED. You're good to go.

Control the LED from IEx

Now you have a fully operational death star, albeit one with a light emitting diode instead of a kyber crystal–powered super-laser array. And what fun is a death star if you can't try it out?

Hook up your Pi to your computer with your micro-USB cable. Shell into it as before with the name circuits@nerves.local and a password of circuits. Now we're ready to use the GPIO interface included with the Circuits Quickstart firmware you burned earlier.

Blink the LED from IEx

Interacting with an LED is pretty simple using the GPIO library. You'll open the pin and grab the reference. Then, you'll write a 1 or 0 to the pin to turn it on or off.

 Frank says:
Why I Built Circuits Quickstart

Circuits Quickstart lets you experiment with hardware right away before you dive into the software. Just install the known working Circuits Quickstart firmware and debug your circuit by interacting with it from IEx. I use it often for one-off experiments.

Let's get to work. Alias the library to save a bit of typing, like this:

```
iex(1)> alias Circuits.GPIO
Circuits.GPIO
```

Now open your pin and grab the reference. Call your reference led, like this:

```
iex(2)> {:ok, led} = GPIO.open(26, :output)
{:ok, #Reference<0.1011226183.268828678.28169>}
```

Excellent. Notice Elixir returned a unique ID called a *reference*. Your reference refers to the open GPIO pin, specifically the one with BCM number 26. You can use that reference to turn on the LED attached to that pin:

```
iex(3)> GPIO.write(led, 1)
:ok
```

Nice! Your LED should be on. If it isn't, unplug your jumper wires, and then tweak your circuit. Maybe your LED is backward, or you've chosen the wrong pins. Plug it back in when you're done, and you'll see your shiny, happy LED:

That's too shiny and happy, but you know how to squash that joy:

```
iex(4)> GPIO.write(led, 0)
:ok
```

And it's blissfully dark again. Now, you can probably imagine what the API might look like once you're ready to organize code. These little virtual light switches we can control with functions are exactly what the doctor ordered. Your circuit is complete, so it's time to wrap up.

What You Built

You built your initial circuit on breadboard that wired up an LED to a temporary circuit board. Breadboard prototyping is a great way to build transient circuits without soldering. The components were LEDs for light, resistors for establishing a safe load, and a couple of wires called jumpers to connect the circuit to the Pi.

Once you connected them, you could control the circuit from IEx. You used the Circuits.GPIO library to write 1s and 0s to a GPIO pin to turn your LED on and off. Now that you've controlled an LED from hardware, you've mastered the "Hello, World" program of the embedded space.

This step seems small, but it's a significant part of the overall project.

Why It Matters

Though a single LED is only a tiny part of the overall project we're building, controlling it demonstrates the primary purpose of Nerves: embedding tiny programs to control hardware devices. Makers control elements in the real world by circuits. Rather than using manual switches and buttons to manipulate the circuits, the IoT relies on interfaces like general-purpose input/output (GPIO). Then Elixir code can manipulate them through existing libraries like Circuits.GPIO.

Now you can put what you learned to work.

Try It Yourself

In this section, you'll expand your circuit to include a few more LEDs and then control them in several ways from the console.

These *easy* problems involve lighting LEDs of different colors.

- Add a second LED, controlled by the same GPIO pin, so that when you write a 1 to the pin, you turn both LEDs on. Make this LED a different color, if you have one.

- Move your second LED to a different GPIO pin so that when you write to an LED, you write them all at the same time.

- Add a third LED to your circuit, on yet a different GPIO pin, and with yet a different color, if you have one.

These *medium* problems involve manipulating a circuit with three LEDS from within IEx.

- Wire three different LEDs that each use different GPIO pins but share the same ground connection.

- With an LED circuit, write an anonymous function in IEx to blink an LED by turning it on, sleeping, and then turning it off.

If you'd like, you can use the Groxio Nerves module[13] videos to help you with some of these exercises. Some of them are available for free, and others are available for purchase.

Next Time

In this chapter, we've focused on building a circuit and controlling it through IEx. Next time, you'll use a program—layer by layer—to control the circuit. When you turn the page, you'll write your first Nerves project.

---

13. https://grox.io/language/nerves/course

Part II

The Working Layered System

With a foundation in place, we'll pick up speed. The next few chapters will build the critical layers of the clock. We'll start with a boundary, an OTP server responsible for working with hardware. Then we'll build the circuits of the clock, wiring up the different LEDs and connecting them to componentry that will ensure that they all light at the same intensity.

Next, we'll build out a core that lets us describe the lights in code, given a time. We'll make some final tweaks to ensure reliability and set the time using some local libraries. The new clock will be ready for display.

Finally, once you have a fully working project, your fun is only beginning. This final chapter gives you the chance to use what you've learned. You'll practice your new skills by building a binary clock based on a custom-printed circuit board.

CHAPTER 4

Blink an LED with Software Layers

In the first chapter, we worked out how to burn firmware. Then we used the Circuits.GPIO library to manipulate a circuit with an LED. In this chapter, we'll build our own firmware to blink an LED with a service layer. We've chosen a simple project in the spirit of achieving small, quick wins. We'll use this tiny project with blinking LEDs to show you how to build a system in layers.

At some point in this chapter, you're probably going to be shaking your head, wondering why you would ever use so many layers to blink one silly LED. When that happens, remind yourself that the goal is to use a *known simple problem*, a blinking LED, to explore a much more complex question: how to build complex hardware projects in layers.

As usual, we'll build up this project in tiny, iterative steps so we can get psychological wins with verified success at every small step. That way, we'll never stray too far from a working system.

At this point, you may be wondering what the right layers are for a hardware project. That's an excellent place to start, so let's get busy!

The Layers of a Nerves Project

Chances are, you're working with Nerves because it's built on a high-level language that gives you features you need, like crash protection and concurrency. In truth, Elixir does make building such systems easier than languages like C because you don't have to write these layers for concurrency and stability yourself. There is a cost to using Nerves, though. You need to understand how the existing Elixir services work to provide the services your project will need. At its core, you're going to be using a feature called OTP.

Embrace OTP

If you haven't already learned about OTP, don't fret. We'll tell you what you need to know. Still, it would pay to put it on your list of things to learn soon. Groxio has a good OTP course[1] to start your journey, and if you're an intermediate Elixir developer wanting to take the next step, check out *Designing Elixir Systems with OTP [IT19]*, a software design book by James Gray II and Bruce Tate. We'll lean heavily on the ideas from those sources.

In *Designing Elixir Systems with OTP [IT19]*, Bruce and James introduce a system for thinking about software layers. The same techniques in that book work on hardware projects as well. Building a system layer by layer is important because adding hardware to a project introduces a new set of challenges to software design. By breaking your system into layers, you only need to deal with one part of the system at any given time, and that really helps you control complexity.

Luckily, you don't have to start with a fully layered system. We'll build a simple program to blink an LED so you can get the hang of the layering system. You can start with only one layer and build from there.

Start with the Layers You Need

We'll use the mental mnemonic in *Designing Elixir Systems with OTP [IT19]*. The first letters in the sentence "Do Fun Things with Big Loud Worker-bees" stand for the layers Data, Functions, Tests; Boundaries, Lifecycles, Workers. Our design is going to follow this pattern pretty closely, starting with the boundary layer. Later on, we'll mix in hardware-specific layers so all of the layers look like the figure shown on page 29.

The diagram has a bold line dividing the *functions* layer and the *boundary* layer. The bottom layers of data, functions, and tests are the *core*, mostly pure functions that are highly predictable and don't interact with code that might fail, like hardware or processes. The secret to good functional programming is to put as much code as possible into a core, where we don't have to worry about complexities like external interfaces, user data, hardware, and process machinery.

The layers on the top of the diagram are the boundaries, lifecycles, and workers. Together, they are the *boundary* and *boundary support*. These boundary layers provide interfaces for common services to the outside world. This layer must manage uncertainty because external services can fail. It is

---

1.   https://grox.io/language/otp/course

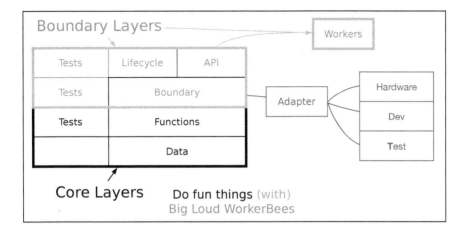

also the chosen layer for interacting with complexity such as process machinery, external services, and hardware, until these services become complex enough to need layers of their own.

The final group of layers are adapters. Each individual adapter represents one *hardware concept* in one *environment*. The hardware concept might be a sensor, a motor, or a simple LED. The context represents a programming environment. Adapters allow separate hardware implementations for test, production, and development builds.

As you might expect, not every program will use every layer, as you can see in the following figure:

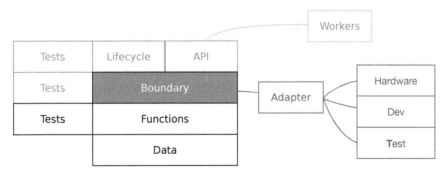

To start with, you don't need a core, but you *will* need the highlighted boundary to access your hardware. That means our initial project will start with a boundary that will access our hardware directly through a library to access an LED. After building that layer, we'll quickly tack on thin layers in the boundary to implement LED access with the features we need.

After we've built our initial boundaries, we'll quickly build on that design. We will extend our boundary to work with adapters for our LEDs. These adapters will let us have a single interface that will wrap a service that's optimally suited to work on either the development machine, a test, or the target hardware.

Frank says:
Layering Improved My Velocity

My coding velocity improved significantly after placing more emphasis on a functional core. Now it seems obvious, but it took several years of Elixir coding to get there. The first few Nerves network config libraries didn't have a layered approach and the software took too long to change because hardware was involved. With the VintageNet networking library for Nerves, I carved out a core and that bought me the time to begin adding features again.

Boundaries and adapters sound like a good amount of work to do for one chapter, so our plan is complete. We've laid out the primary concepts, so we're ready to, um, mix a foundation.

Initialize a Nerves Project from Scratch

You've controlled a single LED with IEx. While that experience was interesting, it really amounts to the world's most awkward light switch. This chapter will focus on making it blink forever, or at least until you get bored. Along the way, we'll explore a coreless design with a hardware layer and a service layer. Because processes and hardware fail, our code is unpredictable and will fit in the boundary.

We're going to build a temporary Nerves project called Blinker for a little experimentation. Later, once we've played with a few important concepts, we'll shift to our permanent project called Clock. For both projects, we'll use Elixir 1.11 and Erlang OTP 23. We'll also use Nerves. Check the following code levels for the versions we're using for this book. For now, install the project and get the system info, like this:

```
$ mix nerves.new blinker
...

Fetch and install dependencies? [Yn] Y
...

$ cd blinker
$ mix nerves.info
...
```

```
Nerves:            1.7.0
Nerves Bootstrap: 1.10.0
Elixir:            1.11.2
```

Perfect. We have our initial project. Now let's go get some dependencies.

Install Target Dependencies

Nerves projects have dependencies too, but there's a slight difference. You'll have some dependencies that run on the host, some that run on all targets, and some that run just on a specific target. Add the GPIO dependency that will control the LED. Change into the blinker directory, and add the circuits_gpio dependency that will blink the LED in the top block of dependencies, like this:

```
defp deps do
  [
    # Dependencies for all targets
    ...
    {:circuits_gpio, "~> 0.4.0"},
    ...
  ]
end
```

Great. Now fetch the dependencies, like this:

```
$ mix deps.get
...
All dependencies are up to date
```

Our dependencies are loaded and ready to go, but not yet for the Pi. To know why, you need to know a little bit about both MIX_ENV and MIX_TARGET. Together, they *determine how a Nerves project is compiled*. MIX_ENV is an atom that describes the environment you're working from, and is usually one of :dev, :test, or :prod. The MIX_TARGET is also an atom. It specifies the name of the hardware target for an Elixir build.

MIX_TARGET

Since compiled code for Nerves projects differs from target to target, mix tasks need a way to determine the hardware platform for a compilation. That's MIX_TARGET, and you'll specify it within an environment variable. If MIX_TARGET is blank, mix will set the value to host. You can access the target with Mix.target/0. Note that unless you include Mix as a dependency, you can only use Mix.target at compile time. To see environments and the default target in action, build without setting MIX_TARGET:

```
$ mix compile
...
Generated blinker app
```

We didn't specify a MIX_TARGET, so the target is :host. Now run tests:

```
$ mix test
...compile...
..
1 doctest, 1 test, 0 failures
```

The tests work fine, and we've compiled two different builds for two different *environments* using mix compile and mix test. That task forced a compilation for the :test environment and a target of :host. Peek into the _build directory:

```
$ ls _build/
dev  test
```

Nice! Each *environment* requires a separate build. As you might expect, each *target* also requires its own build. Let's try out builds for a specific MIX_TARGET, other than :host.

Build the Target Application

We need to pick a target for our Pi Zero, but what target should we specify? It turns out there's a list of targets at Nerves targets.[2] You should see the Raspberry Pi Zero on the list. Get dependencies for our Pi Zero by using MIX_TARGET=rpi0, like this:

```
$ MIX_TARGET=rpi0 mix deps.get
...
  => Success
```

We fetched dependencies before, but since we didn't have a target, the dependencies were solely for the host. Now Nerves has the dependencies it needs, and we can build firmware:

```
$ MIX_TARGET=rpi0 mix firmware
Building ...
```

Success! Notice our MIX_TARGET=rpi0 statement. If we wanted to, we could export the environment variable, and it would stay set for a single window until we changed it. To avoid confusion, we'll explicitly set the target before running any mix command. Let's find out what's in the _build directory:

```
$ ls _build/
dev   rpi0_dev  test
```

---

2. https://hexdocs.pm/nerves/targets.html

Interesting. We ran mix firmware with a specific target. Each build name has a *suffix* showing the environment, and a *prefix* defining the target, with one exception. There is no prefix for :host. There's one build directory for each target-environment combination. Host builds don't have a prefix, but all other targets do. The file names have the form target_environment. That means rpi0_dev is built for the Pi Zero, in development mode. Now we're ready to burn firmware.

Run Our Firmware

In the last chapter, you burned existing firmware from the Circuits Quickstart project. Plug in a microSD card with data you can afford to lose into the slot. Remember, no Grandma Jo heirloom photos! The contents of this card will be replaced. Once you've inserted your card, burn your firmware like this:

```
$ MIX_TARGET=rpi0 mix firmware.burn
...
Success!
Elapsed time: 11.643 s
```

It worked! Now, you can move the microSD card into your Raspberry Pi and throw in the LED circuit. Then you can shell in, like this:

```
$ ssh nerves.local
...
iex(1)> {:ok, led} = Circuits.GPIO.open(26, :output)
{:ok, #Reference<0.3346149684.268566539.51086>}
iex(2)> Circuits.GPIO.write(led, 1)
:ok
iex(3)> Circuits.GPIO.write(led, 0)
:ok
iex(4)>
```

If your SSH keys are not password protected, you might be surprised that you didn't have to type a password. This flow is authenticating through your SSH keys, the ones Nerves installed as part of the build. Now we have a working project that we can build ourselves. Still, we can do better. You still have to keep moving your microSD card, and that's a pain. Let's fix that.

Nerves lets you short-circuit that process with mix upload. Tweak the program with a minor change and upload it again by adding a new function to lib/blinker.ex, like this:

```
def hello2 do
  "Updated!"
end
```

Now you can build your firmware with mix, and then wait a minute or two and use mix to upload it:

```
$ MIX_TARGET=rpi0 mix firmware
...
$ MIX_TARGET=rpi0 mix upload
...
Success!
```

Nice! We no longer need to move the microSD card. Notice Nerves is using partition B because Nerves switches between partitions A and B. That way, if something goes wrong, Nerves can restore the previous deployment! If your SSH keys are password protected, you'll need to build an upload script[3] to upload your firmware instead of using the mix upload task, but the premise remains mostly the same.

Frank says:
Partitions

Though we didn't have enough space to cover them, partitions are a core feature of Nerves. We use them to enable reliable firmware updates and also local storage, believe it or not. If you want to know more, you can check out our hexdocs documentation[a] for a more detailed description about this important feature.

a.   https://hexdocs.pm/nerves/advanced-configuration.html#partitions

Shell into it with the usual ssh nerves@nerves.local, and run Blinker.hello2. You'll get the result from the new Blinker.hello/0, so our program is working. That will streamline things a bit.

We haven't written any code yet, but believe me, these setup steps will pay big dividends. We'll be able to push out our firmware over the wire, and that improved flow will help us work at a higher velocity.

It's finally time to write some boundary code.

Build a Coreless Boundary

After establishing a quick win to burn firmware over the wire, we can move on to the next quick win. We shouldn't ignore our hardware a moment longer.

We'll build a service layer to blink an LED. We want quick wins, so we're going to go with the lightest possible solution to make this project work. Let's prune

---

3.   https://elixirschool.com/en/lessons/specifics/nerves/

the typical layers of a system away until only the minimal ones are left. The following figure shows our coreless design, leaving only a boundary:

As the figure shows, sometimes the libraries we use can build stubs that take the place of a functional core. So it is with the Circuits.GPIO library. When working on a target, it interacts with GPIO pins. When working on the host, it uses pure functions that serve as defacto functional cores.

We'll use two skinny boundary layers. One will control an LED, and the other will blink the LED at regular intervals. Eventually, it might make sense to build multiple versions of the LED layer for the hardware, test, and host builds. For now, we're going to be content with two simple boundary layers, starting with the one for hardware.

Build an LED Without an Adapter or Core

Start a tiny boundary layer to control a single LED in lib/blinker/led.ex by keying this program in:

```
defmodule Blinker.LED do
  alias Circuits.GPIO
```

We start with a Blinker.LED module. This ceremony declares the module and aliases the library we'll need to manipulate our hardware. Our strategy is to build software using a pattern called Constructor-Reducer-Converter (CRC). Similar patterns are used often in user interface development, such as the state reducer pattern[4] by Kent Dodds in Redux. CRC is a simplified version of the state-reducer pattern.

Bruce says:
CRC in the Core

When James Gray II and I wrote *Designing Elixir Systems with OTP [IT19]*, we organized our core and test code a specific way, but we didn't put a name to it. Since I put the CRC name to a ubiquitous Elixir organization pattern, CRC has completely unlocked the way I teach Elixir because reduce/3 is everywhere. I can show students how clean functional cores embracing CRC plug straight into Nerves, OTP, LiveView, and more.

---

4. https://kentcdodds.com/blog/the-state-reducer-pattern-with-react-hooks

CRC has functions which work to produce a datatype with a constructor, transform it with a reducer, and consume it with a converter. You'll lean on that pattern, starting with a constructor:

```
def open(pin) do
  message("Opening #{pin}")
  {:ok, led} = GPIO.open(pin, :output)
  led
end
```

Constructors transform inputs into a piece of data of a common type that's convenient for transformations. In this case, we transform a GPIO pin number into an LED.

Along the way, we write a message to inform the user of what's happening. If it doesn't work, we'll crash, which is what we want our boundary to do because we can't take any more meaningful action.

The function will return a reference, which is a unique ID the GPIO uses to represent an LED. Let's write the next kind of function, two reducers to turn the light on and off:

```
def on(led) do
  message("On: #{inspect(led)}")
  GPIO.write(led, 1)
  led
end

def off(led) do
  message("Off: #{inspect(led)}")
  GPIO.write(led, 0)
  led
end
```

Reducers[5] are functions that both accept and return an argument of a common type called an accumulator. Reducers can also accept other arguments as well. The reducer can transform the accumulator, applying any inbound arguments.

Our functions are reducers in name only, because they both accept and return the led accumulator without transforming it at all. Instead of transforming the accumulator, our reducers exist to apply side effects, namely turning LEDs on or off. Don't be discouraged, though. Later, we'll implement proper reducers that actually track the state of an LED.

---

5. https://redrapids.medium.com/learning-elixir-its-all-reduce-204d05f52ee7

We provide an additional reducer called set/2 that will make it easier for us to set the state of an LED based on data in a program.

Let's look at a private function we'll use to tell us what's happening on the host, if we're running on the host in a development setting:

```
def message(message) do
  # Warning: IO.puts in hardware can be unpredictable
  IO.puts(message)
end
end
```

We print a message using IO.puts/1. Be careful! When you're working with hardware, it's usually not a great idea to use IO.puts/1 because it's not always clear where this output will go. We'll stick with puts briefly to get something up quickly.

Believe it or not, we're already ready to try out what we've done, and we don't need to burn any firmware to do it. Open up IEx with iex -S mix, and you can interact with the new LED, like this:

```
iex(1)> alias Blinker.LED
Blinker.LED
iex(2)> 26 |> LED.open |> LED.on |> LED.off
Opening 26
On: #Reference<0.1490711576.2261909530.152694>
Off: #Reference<0.1490711576.2261909530.152694>
#Reference<0.1490711576.2261909530.152694>
```

Nice! Our constructors and reducers make it easy to work with Elixir pipes, and our boundary layer works on the host. The pipeline on line 2 shows the shape of a typical CRC API. We can produce scripted code flows that marvelously show the intent of what we're doing. If anything fails, we just let it crash. Think of the pipe in this form:

```
inputs |> constructor |> reducer |> reducer |> converter
```

Constructors start with disjointed inputs and shape them into an accumulator for our module. Think of an accumulator as a piece of data of a known type in a convenient form for computation. Our accumulator is an LED struct. The reducers transform the data in some way. In boundary layers, reducers can have side effects, like turning an LED off or on. Converters convert reducers to convenient types we can use in some other way. An example of a universal converter is inspect/1.

We've described a typical Elixir pipeline. When we build code in this shape, Elixir rewards us.

Now you can apply some of what you have learned! Take this opportunity to build this program for the rpi0 target using MIX_TARGET=rpi0 mix firmware. Then you can upload the firmware with mix upload and use ssh to access your target. Then, control your Pi with your LED circuit. All you need to type is 26 |> Blinker.LED.open |> Blinker.LED.on to turn on an LED waiting on BCM pin 26.

When you've done that much, we'll begin working on another boundary layer.

Build a Blinker Boundary

This section with an awesomely alliterative title will build a boundary on top of our LED layer to blink an LED one time, and then multiple times. Rather than put all of the functionality of our program in one place, we're going to separate the parts that know how to communicate with hardware from the parts that know how to blink. You probably won't be surprised to learn that in this section we're going to use a GenServer.

 Bruce says:
Did You Try Turning It Off and On Again?

Customer support representatives are famous for asking users to turn appliances or devices off and on again. Whether you're troubleshooting a cable device or a new electric car, you have likely encountered these instructions.

Elixir's OTP is a library for running generic services in a way that's concurrent, distributed, and resilient. Elixir is famous for reliability because of OTP. When services experience problems, we let them crash and start them in a fresh starting state. OTP is Elixir's way of asking, "Did you try turning it off and on again?"

The lib/blinker/server.ex file will have the service boundary, and it will look like this:

```
defmodule Blinker.Server do
  alias Blinker.LED
  defstruct [:led, :on, :ticker]
  use GenServer
  @pin 26
```

At the top of each file is a bit of ceremony, but this code is doing a lot of work. We alias our LED and define the structure that will make up the state of the GenServer. The led is the representation for a hardware GPIO pin, the :on is the current state, and the :ticker is a function to send the next blink. You could imagine this struct having a count integer to track the number of blinks, but we'll keep this program simple.

Let's build the startup machinery, including a constructor to make dealing with options simple:

```elixir
def new(opts) do
  %__MODULE__{
    on: false,
    led: LED.open(opts[:pin] || @pin),
    ticker: opts[:ticker] || &wait/0
  }
end

def start_link(opts \\ []) do
  GenServer.start_link(__MODULE__, opts, name: __MODULE__)
end

def init(opts \\ []) do
  send(self(), :blink)
  {:ok, new(opts)}
end

def wait, do: Process.send_after(self(), :blink, 1000)
```

We have a new constructor that creates the state for the GenServer. Notice we have convenient defaults for every argument but preserve flexibility by making each option configurable. The start_link/3 function starts the process, naming it _MODULE_ so we'll be able to use the Server name instead of the pid. We also provide the init function to send the initial :blink message and return the initial state of the GenServer.

The wait/0 function will wait a bit of time before triggering the next :blink. Notice that we make this function configurable in the :ticker argument because our tests will be more useful if they don't always have to send messages or sleep.

Now, let's provide the API and implementation of the :blink message.

```elixir
  def handle_info(:blink, blinker) do
    blinker.ticker.()
    {:noreply, blink(blinker)}
  end

  defp blink(%{on: true}=blinker) do
    LED.on(blinker.led)
    %{blinker| on: false}
  end
  defp blink(%{on: false}=blinker) do
    LED.off(blinker.led)
    %{blinker| on: true}
  end
end
```

The handle_info/2 function processes a single :blink by sending the next blink message and calling the blink/1 function to do the bulk of the work. The individual blink/1 functions match on whether the light is on or off. Then they call the appropriate LED functions to turn the light off or on and return a new blinker with a toggled blinker.on field.

It's a short program with a complex flow, but since we manage the complexity one layer at a time, the code is remarkably easy to follow.

Test Drive the Simple Blinker

Let's fire it up. Start iex -S mix without a target to run on the host, or recompile if it's already open. Then exercise the blinker, like this:

```
iex(2)> alias Blinker.Server
iex(3)> Server.start_link
Opening 26
Off: #Reference<0.4070557734.2003697698.10599>
{:ok, #PID<0.273.0>}
On: #Reference<0.4070557734.2003697698.10599>
Off: #Reference<0.4070557734.2003697698.10599>
On: #Reference<0.4070557734.2003697698.10599>
Off: #Reference<0.4070557734.2003697698.10599>
```

It works! It's pretty nice that we can test things without burning firmware because we're already confident that our LEDs work. The development time messages give us reasonable confidence that our blinker is working because they are triggering the right message at the right time.

Now, you already know how to burn firmware. It's almost going to be anticlimactic because you've already verified that you can blink your LED module from the host and that the LED module can control the physical circuit. With a MIX_TARGET of rpi0, run mix firmware, run mix upload, and then shell into your device with mix nerves.local, like this:

```
Blinker.Server
iex(3)> Server.start_link
```

And, as shown in the figure on page 41, the light mercifully blinks!

The blinking is simple, but the time honored computer-controlled flashing is almost enough to make a budding maker weep for joy. It's time to wrap up.

What You Built

In this chapter, you spent a good deal of time working with our software layers without ever touching a circuit. To control complexity, you focused on two tiny *boundary* layers. The first layer focused on LEDs and the second on

blinking. More specifically, the LED was a *hardware* layer that focused on the GPIO interface, and the second was a *process* layer that focused on timing.

This project is probably overkill for something as simple as a blinking LED, but we had a greater goal in mind. The layers of a simple project will inform our decisions when more complex projects come along.

Why It Matters

Building Nerves projects one layer at a time sets you up for success. Boundary layers make a good starting point. The two most common kinds of boundary layers in Nerves are service and hardware layers. Hardware layers isolate hardware interfaces, keeping that complexity in one place. Service layers isolate process machinery that controls timing and tracks state.

Now it's time to put those ideas to use.

Try It Yourself

These *easy* problems involve extending the Blinker API layer.

- Make your LEDs blink slower or faster.
- Change the start_link/0 function to take a duration argument.
- Change your LED and program to use a different GPIO pin.

These *medium* problems involve working with a circuit with multiple LEDs.

- Build a circuit that supports more than one LED, with each LED on a different GPIO pin.

- Build a circuit that supports two LEDs in sequence.

- Build an API to blink more than one LED at the same time, assuming the LEDs are on different GPIO pins.

Next Time

In this chapter, we've focused on building a coreless boundary layer. Next time, we'll shift back to circuits, building the initial circuit for the clock. When you turn the page, be ready to dive back into hardware!

CHAPTER 5

Build the Clock's Circuit

This is the part of the project that all hardware lovers crave. You'll be planning and building the hardware that will make up the clock. It's the shortest part of the book but might take the longest to execute depending on how much experience you have.

For the first time, we'll use a constant current LED driver. Since that much is a mouthful, we'll sometimes refer to it as a constant current driver, or even driver. Here's what it does.

As you work in this chapter, you'll work inside a new mix project called Clock. It will have the implementation for the entire binary clock. Like software, hardware systems are built in layers. The interfaces between the layers make it easy to isolate services and let engineers focus on one bit of complexity at any given time. The TLC5947 chip we bought in Chapter 3, Build a Circuit, on page 15 has the constant current driver that will take care of lighting the LEDs all at once, so all we need to do is attach the LEDs to the TLC5947 board and the TLC5947 board to the Pi.

Here's what the clock face of our project looks like:

The only user interface the user will see is a series of LEDs. We'll mount them in a cabinet by drilling eighteen 5/16-inch holes. Seventeen of the holes will hold live LEDs and one will be a dead LED that we present for symmetry. The clock will tell time using a binary number system.[1] We'll use one of those LEDs to represent an AM/PM indicator, six bits for the second and minute digits, and four bits for the hour.

When we're done, the user will see only the tips of the LEDs, and we'll connect those wires to our device. Let's plan our attack.

Plan the Hardware

You might be tempted to try to control all of your LEDs from the GPIO pins from the Pi. The problems with that approach are twofold. First, there might be too much power for our project to accommodate. Second, the brightness would probably be uneven, and you might even see some flickering. For this reason, our days of simple GPIO pins are over for this project.

Instead of hooking up resistors and LEDs to individual pins, we'll invite an intermediary onto the scene to control things, like a traffic cop. The Pi will give the intermediary specific instructions for turning on and off groups of LEDs and leave it to the traffic cop to carry out the instructions. Our traffic cop is the standardized interface you first encountered in Chapter 3, Build a Circuit, on page 15. This chip uses a standardized hardware interface called SPI, for *Serial Peripheral Interface*, shown in the following figure.

Each of the holes in the previous figure is a potential connection. The two rows with two holes each, labeled 0–23, are potential devices. We'll connect LEDs to seventeen of them. The two rows of holes on each end represent the input and output connections. We'll connect the inputs to the Pi. If you

---

1. https://www.mathsisfun.com/binary-number-system.html

wanted to connect more than the 24 LEDs this project requires, you'd chain the outputs from this chip to the inputs of another.

Since we only need one chip, we'll hook up the constant current driver to the Pi, and the LEDs to the driver, and we'll tell the driver to do the work through a library called Circuits.SPI.

That means the hardware side of this project is tedious, but manageable. First, you'll prepare the constant current driver that will serve as the traffic cop. You'll solder headers to the chip so that you can easily make connections with simple jumper wires. When you're done, you'll have an interface board that's ready to accept LEDs and the individual connections to the Raspberry Pi.

Next, you'll connect the constant current driver to the Pi. This step will go quickly because the SPI interface our driver uses is a common hardware interface, so the connections between the chips are well defined. We'll just follow a known schematic that tells us precisely which pins on each chip to connect with jumper wires.

Frank says:
The Value of Datasheets

Working with this constant current driver was great. We didn't have an exact chip in mind. We just went to AdaFruit and searched for a constant current driver for LEDs. Then we downloaded the TLV5947 datasheet, which documented the messages we needed to make in Elixir. I just had to tell Bruce where to put the standard connections on the Raspberry Pi and point him at the Circuits.SPI documentation, and everything worked right out of the box.

Next, you'll build four individual LED groups representing hours, minutes, seconds, and AM/PM bits. You'll use jumper ribbon wires so we can exert just a little control over the inevitable rat's nest of wires. It's a tedious build because each LED has two wires, and seventeen LEDs means we're soldering 34 joints. You'll plug each LED strip onto the header pins you added to the constant current driver.

Finally, before you build a cabinet and install the LEDs, you'll test the hardware. When you're done, you'll have a completed clock that lacks only working firmware. Let's start the hardware assembly with the constant current driver.

Prepare the Constant Current Driver

The TLC5947 will need several connections. There are many ways to solder together persistent connections. You might decide to solder individual components right onto the TLC5947, but that process is error prone, leading to hard-to-find bugs. Instead, you'll use a more forgiving approach. You'll solder on permanent header pins. That way, you can slide temporary jumper wires onto those headers to make connections. The compromise is a temporary connection, but one that's easy to correct should you make mistakes.

Solder on the Headers

You will need to solder five headers to the board. One six-pin header will cover the inputs, and two long headers will cover each row of LED connections. When you're done, your headers should have long pins protruding from the side of the board that has the chips.

If you've never soldered before, you might want to practice a bit. Try watching a video[2] to get the basics. Make sure you don't have any extra solder between the pins that might cause a short.

Start with the short six-pin header. The board comes with two short headers. You only need one of them. Insert the short pins through the top of the board. Then, use some masking tape or scotch tape to temporarily hold them in place while you turn the board over and solder them up. Alternatively, place the header pins in breadboard, long pins down. Then place the chip upside down over the header pins. Gravity will hold it all in place as you solder it up.

Next, you'll solder on the long boards. The long headers will be too long and will have too many pins. Cut off fifteen or sixteen pins, and remove every fourth pin to leave four groups of three pins, as in the following figure.

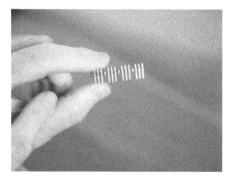

2.   https://learn.adafruit.com/how-to-solder-headers

Next, insert each of the modified headers into the top of the board, tape them in place, and solder them up. When you're done, you should have four rows of headers running left to right in groups of three, and six pins on your left.

Once you've done that much, you're ready to solder the LEDs to the jumper ribbons.

Build Each LED Wire

When you built your initial LED circuit, you had to add resistors to the circuit. Luckily, this board has onboard resistors to do that work, so your only task will be to add length to the LEDs with wires so they're long enough to reach from the constant current driver to the cabinet.

We're going to start with six blue LEDs for minutes. To keep the wires from getting too messy, use ribbon wires for this part of the project. Attach one seven-wire ribbon to the + side of the second LEDs, with an unused wire between two groups of three, and another seven-wire ribbon to the - side. Remember, the + side of the LED is the long end, so don't lose track! Mark the + ribbon of each set with a marker or some tape. The following image shows how we'll group the ribbon wires.

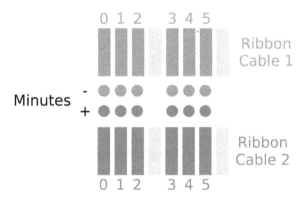

Usually, you can remove the caps of female ribbon connectors by pulling out a tab from the side of the cable and slipping the connector off. Do this to the six wires you need to prepare. If you want, slide a bit of heat shrink[3] onto each LED to insulate the circuit. Then you can slide on an LED (making sure to remember the long legs are positive) and solder up the connection to make it secure. Then cover the bare connection with heat shrink or some electrical tape. If you're using colored heat shrink, it's good to color code your connections to the long positive or short ground legs. In the USA, we often use black

---

3. https://www.adafruit.com/product/4559

and red for + and green for ground, but there's no safety risk for voltages this low, so use the color that works best for you.

When you've done both sides of the second grouping, move on to six green LEDs for the minute grouping, four red LEDs for the hour grouping, and a single LED for the AM/PM grouping. When you're done, if you're using heat shrink, your LED wires should look something like this:

When you're done, you're ready to wire up the project.

Finish the Hardware

The last step to having a working clock is to wire up the project. There are two major connections to make. The LEDs will go on the long headers of the constant current driver. You'll connect the Pi with six more female-to-female jumpers. This process should go quickly.

Then you'll test it. Your tests will make sure there are no major shorts, that your LEDs are correctly aligned, and that your TLC5947 has the right connections.

The first step is to connect your constant current driver to your Pi. If you look closely at the TLC5947, you'll see that the input pins are labeled. This table will show how to build your connections.

Pi Pin Name	Pi Pin Number	TLC5947 Pin Name
5v Power	2	V+
Ground	6	GND
SPI0 MOSI / COPI	19	DIN
SPI0 SCLK	23	CLK
-	-	/OE
SPI0 CE0	24	LAT

Hook up the pins in the previous table using Pinout[4] to double check the Pi orientation and pin numbers.

Next, connect the LEDs. Keep in mind that the ground pins closest to the center of the board connect to the short LED legs, and the power pins on the outside of the board connect to the positive, long legs according to the following diagram:

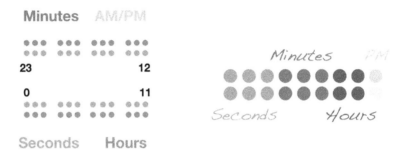

Note that the pins go in a horseshoe shape in a counter-clockwise direction beginning with 0 on the lower left and ending with pin 23 on the upper left.

All that remains is to test the hardware and then build the cabinet of your dreams.

Test the Hardware and Build the Cabinet

Soon, it will be time to build out your glorious cabinet, but before you do anything permanent, it's best to test what you have built so far. We will handle the test in two parts. First, we'll generate our new Nerves project with the circuits_spi dependency, and then we'll use the interface to turn on some lights.

Let's test the system now.

Build a Networked Project

To test the project, we're going to need a new Nerves project. Luckily, you already know how to create those. We'll throw in a new wrinkle to connect it to the network, and then we'll be done.

Create a new project with mix nerves.new clock:

```
$ mix nerves.new clock
```

---

4. https://pinout.xyz/pinout/i2c

Next, fetch dependencies. Add these two dependencies for working with our circuits and setting time zones:

```
# all
{:tzdata, "~> 1.1"},
{:circuits_spi, "~> 0.1"},
```

While you're at it, open mix.lock to make sure you have vintage_net_wifi of 0.9.2 or greater so you can access a new network configuration feature. Follow the same steps we did in the first chapter. With a target of rpi0:

- Build and burn firmware with mix firmware and mix firmware.burn.
- Shell into the Pi over your USB connection with ssh nerves.local.

Now you'll have a working project that's connected to your host. Configure your network, like this:

```
iex> VintageNetWiFi.quick_configure("ssid", "password")
```

Omitting the password for an open network works too. This quick-start tool usually makes it pretty easy to set up your network. Still, attaching your device to your home wireless might not go as expected. Let's look at a few quick tools that might help.

Debug and Tailor Your Connection

If you're not using an access point with WPA2 enabled, see the VintageNet Cookbook[5] for other common configuration use cases. After you've done so, keep in mind that after booting, VintageNet keeps trying to connect. If something is wrong such as a typo in the SSID or password, running RingLogger.next can sometimes provide hints.

If you need a more sophisticated connection or your VintageNet doesn't yet support quick_configure/2, check out the excellent docs[6] for VintageNet, the networking service for Nerves.

From now on, your Pi will boot up with wireless access *and it will fetch the right time.*

We need to do one more thing. We'll push out some bytes to our SPI.

Test the SPI

It turns out that we need to push out some bytes representing 12-bit brightnesses for each of the 24 LEDs supported by the SPI interface. So we'll open

---

5.   https://hexdocs.pm/vintage_net/cookbook.html
6.   https://hexdocs.pm/vintage_net_wifi/readme.html

the SPI interface, build a list of 24 12-bit words using binaries, and transmit those to the SPI.

Open up the bus first:

```
iex> Circuits.SPI.bus_names
["spidev0.0", "spidev0.1"]
iex> Circuits.SPI.open "spidev0.0"
{:ok, #Reference<0.1505575749.270139404.70378>}
iex> {:ok, spi} = v(3)
{:ok, #Reference<0.1505575749.270139404.70378>}
```

We get a list of busses and guess that the first one will work. Then we open it and pick up the reference with a pattern match.

Now build a couple of binaries to transfer to your circuit. To turn lights on, the binary will have 24 words in the form <<0xfff::12>>. To turn lights off, we'll need 24 words of <<0x000::0>>. We can build both quickly with for comprehensions, like this:

```
iex(11)> on = for _x <- 1..24, into: <<>>, do: <<0xfff::12>>
<<255, 255, 255, 255, 255, 255, 255, 255, 255, 255, 255, 255, 255, ...>>
iex(12)> off = for _x <- 1..24, into: <<>>, do: <<0x000::0>>
<<0, 0, 0, 0, 0, 0, 0, 0, 0, 0, 0, 0, 0, 0, 0, 0, 0, 0, 0, 0, 0, 0, ...>>
```

Elixir's binaries make dealing with individual bytes a breeze. Now we can control the circuit by using Circuits to transfer them to the clock via SPI, like this:

```
iex> Circuits.SPI.transfer spi, off
{:ok,...}
iex> Circuits.SPI.transfer spi, on
{:ok,...}
```

Hopefully, your code turns your LEDs on and off. If not, you may need to tweak your circuit. If *some* of the LEDs light up but some don't, your constant current driver is working. If *none* of them light up, you might check the connections to the TLC5947 and make sure your LEDs are all in the right direction. You already know how to flash a single LED, so you can test any of your individual LEDs if needed with GPIO.

For now, we'll claim victory and move on.

Build the Cabinet

Once you've tested out your project, you can build a cabinet and install it, should you decide to do so.

We're not going to tell you how to build your cabinet, but we will give you a few ideas. Your cabinet will depend on the materials you know how to use and your skills with those materials. Frank and Bruce each prefer different cabinets for this project. Frank uses a laser cutter to build specialized cases in plastics, and Bruce prefers working with wood. Either way, we'll give you a few simple guidelines.

The way you present your clock face is up to you. If you add an LED that's always off, you can build a 2x9 display like the one we've shown. You could also build a 3x6 grid with seconds and minutes each on their own row and the hours sharing a row with the AM/PM indicator. Regardless of what you choose, you will probably want to use 5/16-inch holes with some plastic LED mounts to hold them in place. The following image has the dimensions of a grid.

1/2 inch
at center

5/16 inch
hole width

When it's time to build the cabinet, simply thread the LEDs through the holes from the back, snap on your plastic LED mount, and seat it firmly in the hole. If friction isn't enough to hold it in place, add a dab of glue. Make sure you leave room for a micro-USB cable in the back of the cabinet to power your project, or a way to install and replace batteries once you're done.

You've worked hard to finish this project. Now it's time to wrap up.

What You Built

This chapter is among the shortest in the book, but the execution may take the longest. We built a circuit based on a Pi with a TLC5947 to light LEDs through a Serial Peripheral Interface (SPI). We soldered on headers and used jumper wires to make connections that were reasonably stable but easy enough to change in case of trouble.

The LEDs were all wired tiny circuits of their own, and each one went to numbered pins on the constant current driver. The connections between the Pi and the TLC5947 used standard pins built for the purpose.

Why It Matters

Hardware engineers use layers the same way software developers do. SPI interfaces isolate hardware components that serve one purpose. Our constant current driver turns LEDs on and off. Since we were able to focus on nothing but attaching LEDs to the board, the project moved more quickly than it otherwise would have.

Now, you can use Circuits.SPI to play with your creation.

Your Turn

These *easy* problems involve turning lights on and off.

- The lights are too bright. If 0xfff is full brightness and 0 is off, find some brightnesses in between that are more pleasing. Note you can use 4095 instead of 0xfff to make it easier.

- What happens if you send only 12 bytes instead of 24? Which bytes do you control, those on the top or the bottom?

This *hard* problem involves building your own circuit with a color LED.

- The outputs for the board are divided into three so they can be used with color LEDs. Control a colored LED with this board. You should be able to set it up with jumpers and the legs of your LED.

Next Time

In the next chapter, you'll put this circuit to work. Since preparing the data you'll send is such a big part of the project, we'll start with a functional core, and we'll wrap the constant current driver in a hardware layer. Then we'll build a GenServer to send the data, based on local time, to the TLC5947.

CHAPTER 6

Write a Clock with a Core

In the last chapter, you made a box of LEDs. In this chapter, you'll turn it into a clock with beautiful motion. Most of the project will use techniques you've seen in this book. Your code will have two boundary layers: one service layer and one hardware layer. The service layer will be a basic GenServer that's thin and simple, as shown in the following figure.

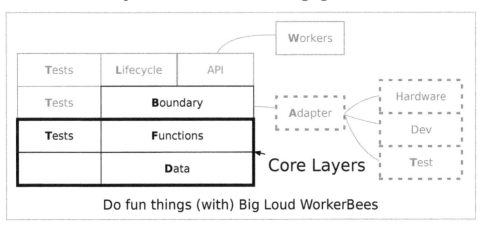

Do fun things (with) Big Loud WorkerBees

The figure shows the boundary layer where the GenServer will be, and also some layers you have not encountered in this book. You'll need a core layer to handle the complex data structure the constant current driver needs to manipulate your LEDs. The layers in the bold box make up the core. You'll also expand the hardware adapter from one module to three modules. One will run on the embedded target, and the other two will run on the host in the development and test environments. Finally, you'll build a lifecycle layer. This supervisor will start the clock's server when Elixir launches the application, and it will pull the correct configuration for your environment.

When you're done, you'll know how to control hardware with single-responsibility software that you can manage, piece by piece. We'll work through the previous figure from the bottom up, starting with the data and functions in the core.

Write the Core

In this chapter, you're going to build onto the clock project you created in Chapter 5, Build the Clock's Circuit, on page 43. If you missed that instruction, go back and create the project now. Once you've done so, we'll start to work on your project's core.

Functional cores express complicated application logic by using convenient data structures and composing functions to transform those structures one small step at a time. Cores control complexity by allowing the simplest compositions, without the need to capture failure. In Elixir programs, cores allow composition with pipes, often using the CRC pattern.

Though our core won't deal with hardware per se, it *will* need to produce data the hardware can consume. Eventually, we'll use a library called Circuits.SPI to integrate with the constant current driver. We'll talk more about Circuits.SPI later. For now, understand that the core must produce *binary data* for hardware, and perhaps some other format for tests and execution in IEx. Keep that in mind as we wrestle with the core.

Core layers work with custom datatypes convenient for intermediate computation. Think of a core's type as an accumulator. The best cores export only functions that either accept or return the core's type. Constructors build an accumulator from convenient inputs. Reducers perform one basic calculation to transform one instance of a type to another instance of that type. Converters translate the core's type to some other type.

Build an Accumulator with a Constructor

Our core's constructor will build an accumulator out of the the typical components of a clock with keys for seconds, minutes, hours, and an ampm indicator. We'll represent each of these as integers, since they are intermediate values that will translate into bits that tests can use or a binary containing bytes that the software interface can consume.

Let's start with the top of the Core module in lib/clock/core.ex:

```
defmodule BinaryClock.Core do
  defstruct ~w[ampm hours minutes seconds]a
  @brightness 0x060
```

It's best to represent the core with the elements of a clock instead of jumping straight to the bits and byte streams the constant current driver will need. The brightness is a three-byte Hex number. Next is the constructor.

Build a Constructor

This constructor will take an Elixir time. To tell what's inside, call Time.utc_now |> Map.keys from within IEx and you'll see the list [:_struct_, :calendar, :hour, :microsecond, :minute, :second]. The minute and second inputs should translate directly, but we'll need to build the ampm indicator and translate the 24-hour clock to a 12-hour clock instead, like this:

```
def new(%{hour: hours, minute: minutes, second: seconds}) do
  %__MODULE__{
    ampm: hours |> div(12),
    hours: hours |> rem(12),
    minutes: minutes,
    seconds: seconds
  }
end
end
```

Perfect. These basic division functions do the trick. Let's try out what we've built so far:

```
iex> alias Clock.Core
iex> time = Core.new Time.utc_now
%Clock.Core{ampm: 1, hours: 3, minutes: 39, seconds: 5}
```

The constructor does exactly what it should. This convenient form is a struct with four integers. When we make the clock components, we'll be able to treat each of the integers in the same way. We'll do that work in a converter layer.

Convert the Times to Bits

We could use dozens of methods to extract ones and zeros from these six integers. This converter will use a mixture of Elixir Integer functions, a for comprehension, and binaries. Add the to_leds/2 to start the ball rolling. The function will take a clock and a format because the hardware layer will eventually need these formats for the development, test, and target adapters. We have a couple of decisions to make about the presentation.

Remember the layout of the clock from the previous chapter. Starting in the lower left, we'll show seconds, hours, ampm, and minutes. We need to decide whether to show the least significant bit first or last. We'll choose to show the least significant bit first, meaning we'll need to reverse the bits from their typical state.

Next, think about the horseshoe shape of the bytes in the TLC5947. Bits 0–11 go left to right as you'd expect, but bits 12–23 will go right to left. That means we'll reverse the first two groupings for seconds and hours but leave the others alone, like this:

```
def to_leds(clock, format \\ :bytes) do
  [
    (clock.seconds |> padded_bits |> Enum.reverse),
    (clock.hours |> padded_bits |> Enum.reverse),
    (clock.ampm |> padded_bits),
    (clock.minutes |> padded_bits)
  ]
  |> List.flatten
  |> formatter(format)
end
```

That works. We list each bit grouping from top to bottom, piped through a few functions, and then pipe the resulting four lists through List.flatten/1 to make one list of bits and then a formatter. We already talked about the Enum.reverse/1 functions, so let's address the padded_bits/ function.

The TLC5947 has 24 bits, so having four groupings of six bits each is perfect. So what do we do if there are not enough bits? For example, the number 3 in binary form is 11. That's not going to work with our clock, because each grouping needs six digits. That means the data will need padding, like this:

```
defp padded_bits(number, total_length \\ 6) do
  bits = Integer.digits(number, 2)
  padding = List.duplicate(0, total_length - length(bits))

  padding ++ bits
end
```

We compute the bits for base 2 using the digits/2 function and then build the padding. The result is the padding plus the bits. That means padded_bits(3) will return [0, 0, 0, 0, 1, 1], which is perfect for our purposes.

For now, let's return a formatter that simply returns its input.

```
defp formatter(list, :none), do: list
```

That form will work fine in a test adapter and will give us a chance to test the code so far. Now, try that much out:

```
iex(3)> time |> Core.to_leds(:none)
[1, 0, 1, 0, 0, 0, 1, 1, 0, 0, 0, 0, 0, 0, 0, 0, 0, 1, 1, 0, 0, 1, 1, 1]
iex(4)> Integer.undigits(Enum.reverse([1, 0, 1, 0, 0, 0]), 2)
5
```

And we have 24 bits represented as 1s and 0s. That's fine for a test, when the most important characteristic is data that's easy to decipher. The tests will be able to quickly determine whether the integers are translated from base 10 to base 2.

Notice the first six bits represent the seconds, a 5. The undigits/2 makes sure the list of bits is the expected 5 base-10 number.

Format Data Two More Ways

Converters translate accumulators, which are convenient for computation, to other types convenient for consumption. The key to building Nerves systems is to build software that works three different ways: on the target hardware, on the development host, and in tests.

Our to_leds/2 function is a converter, and it uses formatter/2 to format the function result to a convenient form. The :none formatter will work in tests, so we need additional formatters. One should format the LEDs nicely for the TLC5947, and the other should print the LEDs nicely in IEx. Start with the hardware version, called :bytes:

```
defp formatter(list, :bytes), do: to_bytes(list)

defp to_bytes(list) do
  for bit <- Enum.reverse(list), into: <<>>, do: to_byte(bit)
end

defp to_byte(0), do: <<0::12>>
defp to_byte(_), do: <<@brightness::12>>
```

This code is remarkably short. The formatter with the matching pattern calls to_bytes/1 with the inbound list. That function goes through the bits, reverses them based on the TLC5947 spec sheet, and converts each bit to a 12-bit word. Then the for comprehension collects those into the stream of words for the Circuits.SPI.

Now, build a version that's easy to read in IEx, like this:

```
defp formatter(list, :pretty), do: pretty(list)

defp to_pretty_byte(0), do: "-"
defp to_pretty_byte(_), do: "*"

defp pretty(list) do
  for bit <- list, into: "", do: to_pretty_byte(bit)
end
```

Make sure you add the formatter/2 function clause right where the existing formatter/2 clauses are located. The code looks similar because it does a similar job. Instead of converting the word into a 12-bit brightness, the to_pretty_byte/1 function converts it to a pretty string. Try the adapter:

```
iex(9)> time |> Core.to_leds(:bytes)
<<...>>
iex(10)> time |> Core.to_leds(:pretty)
"*-*---**--------**--***"
iex(11)>
```

If you do the binary math, you'll find that the values are correct. Now that the code can produce a string of bytes that the hardware needs, you're ready to code the hardware adapters.

Adapters Run One System, Three Ways

The first boundary that interacts with hardware is an *abstraction layer* called an *adapter*. These layers let programmers present one interface and multiple implementations. The goal is to have one program that runs in three places with as little disruption as possible.

If you wanted to, you could add a bit of compiler safety with a behaviour.[1] We're going to leave the behaviour implementation to you. Because Elixir is a dynamically typed language, all you technically need to do is provide adapter modules that present functions with the same names and arities.

Each of the adapters will handle a different use case. The test layer needs individual bits, the hardware layer needs binaries that work with Circuits.SPI, and the development layer needs to show pretty strings that represent the clock face.

Bruce says:
My Nerves Breakthrough

I took an initial pass at Nerves four years before I wrote this book but had a difficult time. Teaching OTP and applying the software layering techniques I taught opened up a whole new world for me. The main lesson was that interfaces allow back ends for the same system. Establishing interfaces for test, development, and production made everything click.

The Circuits.SPI interface we'll use for the target is based on a concept called a *bus*. Busses potentially have multiple devices, and a software layer must open one to interact with it, much like a file in an operating system. That means

---

1. https://embedded-elixir.com/post/2018-09-25-mocks-and-explicit-contracts-expansion/

each adapter will need a *constructor* function to open the adapter. Then, each function will need a converter to present the LED pattern to the user. Let's start with the target.

The Target Adapter

We'll make the adapters structs so they'll have the actual module built in as the _struct_ key.[2] The target adapter must physically open the bus and send the bytes representing the clock face. In lib/clock/adapter/target.ex, build the constructor first:

```
defmodule Clock.Adapter.Target do
  defstruct [:time, :spi]
  alias Clock.Core
  alias Circuits.SPI

  def open(bus, time) do
    :timer.send_interval(1_000, :tick)

    bus = bus || hd(SPI.bus_names())
    {:ok, spi} = SPI.open(bus)
    %__MODULE__{time: time, spi: spi}
  end
```

The constructor will need the spi reference and the time. The open/2 function opens the bus and returns the adapter with the time and spi keys. Next, present the bytes to the user, like this:

```
  def show(adapter, time) do
    adapter
    |> Map.put(:time, time)
    |> transfer()
  end

  defp transfer(adapter) do
    bytes = adapter.time |> Core.new |> Core.to_leds(:bytes)
    SPI.transfer(adapter.spi, bytes)
    adapter
  end
end
```

We add the time to the adapter, and then send the adapter to a private function to transfer the bytes via Circuits.SPI using the data we build from the core. We return the adapter so the server will have the last time presented for debugging purposes.

Pausing quickly to test this function makes sense:

---

2. https://elixir-lang.org/getting-started/structs.html

```
iex> a = Target.open "bus", Time.utc_now |> Target.show(Time.utc_now)
%Clock.Adapter.Target{
  spi: #Reference<0.862938587.3806461979.14092>,
  time: ~T[20:10:31.306738]
}
```

It appears to be working. Take the time to revel in your work. Build and push firmware to the target, and you'll be able to shell out to the Pi and display the time with LEDs. Do a brief happy dance, and then we'll build a test layer.

The Test Adapter

The testing adapter will look much like the target one, with a couple of exceptions. First, there's no need to open an adapter. Second, rather than translating bytes, it makes more sense to add the bits to the adapter, so a test case could conceivably collect a few ticks and check the values using a strategy called *mocking*.

The lib/clock/adapter/test.ex file tells the story:

```
defmodule Clock.Adapter.Test do
  defstruct [:time, bits: []]
  alias Clock.Core

  def open(_bus \\ nil, time \\ Time.utc_now) do
    %__MODULE__{time: time}
  end
```

The defstruct across the adapters does not have to match. This one has a bits part to accumulate consecutive clock readings. There's no need for a spi key because we're not connected to hardware, so open/3 simply returns the time with the default values and moves on.

Now, let's show the results reducer:

```
  def show(adapter, time) do
    adapter
    |> Map.put(:time, time)
    |> concat
  end

  defp concat(adapter) do
    bits = adapter.time |> Core.new |> Core.to_leds(:none)
    %{adapter| bits: [bits| adapter.bits]}
  end
end
```

The only difference is the concat/1 function that tracks bits from the Core in the adapter accumulator. When you write test cases as an exercise, you'll use this bit to click your clock through a couple of cycles and make sure that show is computing bits correctly.

Testing this adapter means writing a test. Put it in test/adapter_test.exs:

```
defmodule AdapterTest do
  use ExUnit.Case
  import Clock.Adapter.Test

  test "Tracks time" do
    adapter =
      open(:unused, ~T[20:13:17.304475])
      |> show(~T[01:02:04.0])
      |> show(~T[01:02:05.0])

    [second, first] = adapter.bits

    assert [0, 0, 1|_rest] = first
    assert [1, 0, 1, 0, 0, 0, 1|_rest] = second
  end
end
```

This is a test of only the Adapter.Test module, but a test of the GenServer would work the same way. Neither of these adapters is convenient for IEx. A development adapter should make it easy to run our project in the console. We'd like to see messages printed or logged when important things happen. We don't care about the hardware because the development mode will run on the host. Let's build a development adapter next.

The Dev Adapter

The dev adapter in lib/clock/adapter/dev.ex will be much like the test adapter but will send a log message rather than adding bits to the console. The ring logger will allow this adapter to work on the Pi for debugging as well. Let's see how it works:

```
defmodule Clock.Adapter.Dev do
  defstruct [:time]
  require Logger
  alias Clock.Core

  def open(_bus \\ nil, time \\ Time.utc_now) do
    :timer.send_interval(1_000, :tick)
    %__MODULE__{time: time}
  end
```

The struct needs a time, but not the spi key. The spi interface is meaningless on the host; the hardware is elsewhere. Still, this adapter is a great place to establish the ticks that will make our GenServer run later. This design will allow for the target and development environments to have a running

GenServer, and the test environment can test the features of the GenServer by explicitly sending tick messages instead of waiting on automated ticks. That way, the tests can be faster but still ensure the integrity of the software layer.

Now, let's see the show/2 reducer.

```
def show(adapter, time) do
  adapter
  |> Map.put(:time, time)
  |> log
end

defp log(adapter) do
  face = adapter.time |> Core.new |> Core.to_leds(:pretty)
  Logger.debug("Clock face: #{face}")
  adapter
end
end
```

This reducer works like the others. It has a custom function to show the clock face. The face is primitive, but it can easily be extended later based on the isolated :pretty formatter in the core. Now try it out:

```
iex> RingLogger.attach
:ok
iex> Clock.Adapter.Dev.open |> Clock.Adapter.Dev.show(Time.utc_now)

07:26:20.889 [debug] Clock face: --*-*------------*-**-*-
%Clock.Adapter.Dev{time: ~T[12:26:20.889926]}
```

It works, showing a friendly clock representation while the logger is attached. You can come back and improve the representation later. The important thing is that we don't need to unpack the binaries to see whether the bits are off or on.

Now let's build the GenServer in the services layer.

Build the Service Layer

Adapters are boundary layers that run on a specified target to control hardware and also in host environments for convenience. With the adapters in hand, the clock is almost complete. It can translate an Elixir time to LEDs upon request. The last problem is making that request at one-second intervals.

Recall that the adapters already send one second :tick messages. The new service layer needs only respond to them.

Build the Service

This GenServer in lib/clock/server.ex will be short and sweet. It will need to keep an adapter, a time zone, and the local time, like this:

```elixir
defmodule Clock.Server do
  defstruct [:adapter, :time, :timezone]
  use GenServer
  @spi_bus_name "spidev0.0"
  @timezone "US/Eastern"
```

We tack on a couple of module attributes with a default time zone and a default SPI bus name. Next, we'll gather that data from inbound options, or convenient defaults:

```elixir
  def init(opts) do
    tz = opts[:timezone] || @timezone
    bus = opts[:spi] || @spi_bus_name

    time = local_time(tz)
    adapter = opts[:adapter] || Clock.Adapter.Dev

    {:ok,
     %__MODULE__{adapter: adapter.open(bus, time), time: time, timezone: tz}}
  end

  defp local_time(timezone) do
    DateTime.now!(timezone, Tzdata.TimeZoneDatabase)
  end
```

This code has no surprises. It serves as the constructor for this service, gathering inputs from the inbound options when they are available and choosing convenient defaults when they are not. It uses those values to build an adapter and get the local time. Then it returns the initial state, an accumulator, for the GenServer.

Next, we'll look at the event handler that serves as the reducer, the handle_info/2 for the :tick message the adapter sent earlier.

```elixir
def handle_info(:tick, server), do: {:noreply, advance(server)}

defp advance(server) do
  module = server.adapter.__struct__
  advanced = module.show(server.adapter, local_time(server.timezone))
  %{server| adapter: advanced}
end
```

With each tick, we advance the state of the clock. The server uses the appropriate adapter to either simulate hardware on the host or light LEDs on the client.

Notice the adapter module. Because the adapter is a struct, there's a key called _struct_ with the module we need. We then use it to call the show/2 reducer, presenting the time data to the user based on the rules in the adapter. Whether the user is working in IEx, viewing the hardware clock face, or running a test, they get exactly what they need. That's the beauty of the adapter. The GenServer layer doesn't need to do anything different for different adapter types. That's the beauty of adapter layers.

Now, shift to the API layer. The only function it needs to support is start_link since the adapters are already sending the :tick messages:

```
  def start_link(opts \\ %{}) do
    GenServer.start_link(__MODULE__, opts, name: __MODULE__)
  end
end
```

The function starts the service with a GenServer.start_link, providing the module with the implementation, the options that will produce the initial state, and a name. Now the clock is fully functional and we can try it out.

Try Your Clock

You can run the service, like this:

```
iex(1)> RingLogger.attach
:ok
iex(2)> Clock.Server.start_link
{:ok, #PID<0.261.0>}

08:24:49.551 [debug] Clock face: *---**---*----------**---
08:24:50.551 [debug] Clock face: -*--**---*----------**---
08:24:49.551 [debug] Clock face: **--**---*----------**---
```

If you track the first few bits on the left, you can see the binary numbers 1, 2, and 3. It's working!

You can also build and push your firmware to try it out on the target, but you'll need to shell into that environment and provide the right configuration:

```
iex> Clock.Server.start_link(adapter: Clock.Adapter.Target)
```

The clock is working, but it has the most annoying on-switch ever built. The user has to plug the device in, wait for it to boot, shell in, and type a cryptic command. Good luck getting your teenager or cleaning service to do that if they kick the plug. Let's fix that.

Manage LifeCycle with a Supervisor

The last layer we need to think about is the lifecycle layer. Luckily, we don't have to write it! OTP already has everything we need as an OTP *supervisor*. Whenever an Elixir OTP project starts, it calls the start/2 function in the existing lib/clock/application.ex file. This start/2 function starts the supervisor for the project, and the supervisor spins up the processes for each boundary layer. As the start name suggests, this function is responsible for starting the application cleanly. Here's what it looks like in our layer diagram:

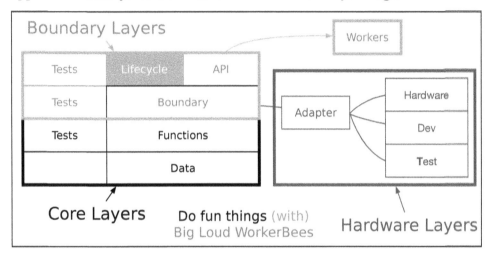

The highlighted layer in the previous figure sits on top of the OTP boundary we built to control the clock. Because most of the lifecycle management details are already implemented by Elxir's OTP libraries, the application.ex implementation will be remarkably simple.

Application.start/2 will start the supervisor for the project. Supervisors manage application startup and shutdown in two cases. The supervisor API cleanly starts up the service processes—implemented by OTP GenServers—when an application starts, takes them down when the application shuts down, and restarts them when a server process crashes. Here's the bit that starts any child services, with comments removed:

```
def start(_type, _args) do
  opts = [strategy: :one_for_one, name: Clock.Supervisor]
  children =
    [] ++ children(target())
  Supervisor.start_link(children, opts)
end
```

This tiny function calls Supervisor.start_link/2 with a list of children. It turns out that the list of children is empty.

Supervisors also come into play when processes crash unexpectedly. When a process exits with an error code, the BEAM notifies supervisors so they shut down all dependent services and then bring them back up in a clean starting state. It usually works, and that's why customer service reps the world over ask, "Did you try turning it off and on again?"

Start the Clock.Server on the Host

For Nerves, supervisors are a bit more complicated. Some children don't work on the hosts, and some don't work on targets. That's why you see the line [] ++ children(target()) in Nerves projects. We'll rely on the children/1 function to start the dependencies. First, we'll make the children start on the host to try out the service. Then we'll move the supervisor to the target. That way, the target clock will start automatically, but you'll be able to turn on the server as required for any of the host environments.

Add a child tuple with default options to application.ex, beneath the children(:host) function head, like this:

```
def children(:host) do
  [{Clock.Server, []}]
end
```

From here on out, when you start the project in any context, Elixir will start the supervisor too. The supervisor will in turn start the binary clock. You don't have to take it on faith, though. You can see the project run using Erlang's observer. To start it, first start your project with IEx -S mix, and then open up IEx, like this:

```
$ iex -S mix
Erlang/OTP 23 [erts-11.0] [source] [64-bit] [smp:12:12]
[ds:12:12:10] [async-threads:1] [hipe]

Compiling 1 file (.ex)
Interactive Elixir (1.11.2) - press Ctrl+C to exit (type h() ENTER for help)
iex(1)> :observer.start
:ok
```

With Observer started, you can click the applications tab. You might have to resize the window to get the applications to appear. Once you do, your observer instance will look like the figure shown on page 69.

Notice the right-hand side. There's a Elixir.Clock.Supervisor and a Elixir.Clock.Server process on the far right. You can get some information about the supervisor's children, including the PID:

```
iex(2)> Supervisor.which_children Clock.Supervisor
[{Clock.Server, #PID<0.257.0>, :worker, [Clock.Server]}]
```

The PID is 257. You can use the observer to kill it by right-clicking the menu or cntl-clicking the Mac, like this:

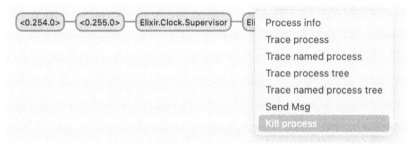

Once you've done so, specify a reason of kill and run the which_children/1 function again:

```
iex(3)> Supervisor.which_children Clock.Supervisor
[{Clock.Server, #PID<0.10570.0>, :worker, [Clock.Server]}]
```

The process ID is new! That means OTP restarted it. Now you can use the RingLogger to verify that things are working smoothly:

```
iex(1)> RingLogger.attach
16:25:03.743 [debug] Clock face: **------*--------*-**--*
16:25:04.743 [debug] Clock face: --*-----*--------*-**--*
16:25:05.743 [debug] Clock face: *-*-----*--------*-**--*
...
```

It started automatically, so we're on the right track. Father Time is finally rolling. When you're ready, shut down IEx and restore the children(:host) to an empty list. In the same way, we'll rely on the supervisor to start the clock on the target.

Start the Clock.Server on the Target

A working clock is so close, you can almost feel it! Starting the clock on the target is slightly more complex. For the Dev adapter, the default options were all fine. The target is different. We need to correctly configure the server. We'll need to specify the target adapter, the time zone, and the SPI bus name.

The target configuration file handles configuration for generic targets, so it's the right place to add specific configuration for the clock. After all, these options are for the hardware implementation. Add these bits to config/target.exs, right below the import Config statement:

```
import Config

config :clock,
  adapter: Clock.Adapter.Target,
  timezone: "US/Eastern",
  spi: "spidev0.0"
```

Later, if we decide to build out another embedded device, that SPI bus name might need to change from target to target, but we'll leave it alone for now. We add the adapter, the time zone, and the SPI bus name, which are all of the data the clock server needs to work. Start the service using that configuration in application.ex, like this:

```
def children(:host) do
  []
end

def children(_target) do
  [{Clock.Server, Application.get_all_env(:clock)}]
end
```

Now build your firmware and upload it. With any luck, your clock will have LEDs cryptically dancing out the correct time. It's a true, um, nerd-vana.

With a fully functional clock that automatically starts with the correct time, there's nothing left to do. It's time to wrap up.

What You Built

This chapter has the entire software layer for the project. The functional core creates time structs with a constructor and converts them to convenient formats for different use cases. The core provides logic for three adapters with identical interfaces but different implementations for hardware, IEx, and tests. Together, these features show time upon request.

The service layer processes periodic requests for time and delegates the task of showing the local time to configurable adapter layers. The lifecycle layer uses supervisors to automatically start the service layer if needed.

Why It Matters

Core layers are important because they express complex logic in pure functions without needing to manage complexity. Adapters allow clients to use the same interfaces to access different implementations without added complexity. Boundaries can use adapters without needing to account for where software is running. Lifecycle layers control the starting and stopping of services.

Taken together, the layers of the clock make something powerful and complicated. Taken apart, you can focus on one small part of the system at a time, as you saw in our frequent IEx diversions. Now you can use these ideas to build features of your own.

Try It Yourself

This *easy* problem involves writing tests for the core layer.

- Write tests for the Core layer. Since this code is in the core, your tests won't need to start or stop GenServers. You also won't need any special setup or teardown code.

This *medium* problem involves testing the GenServer layer.

- Write tests for the GenServer. It might make sense to start the GenServer without sending periodic messages to it and advance the clock automatically with send(self(), :tick) messages.

This *medium* problem involves building a behaviour.

- Build a behaviour for the adapters. You might be able to abstract some of the common behaviour within the show/2 function.

These *hard* problems allow extension of features on the clock.

- Use an ambient light sensor like the veml6030[3] to control the brightness on your clock.

- Set the brightness on your clock according to the current time. At night-time, dim the clock.

What's Next?

This Nerves project is a great way to experiment with Elixir software design as you work with bits and bytes to set the state of a clock. By building your software in layers, you can isolate pure functions in the core, manage uncertainty in the boundary, and relegate lifecycle support to the configuration and supervision code.

You can see the benefits as you move from one layer to the next. For example, the clock has the sophistication of self-healing through OTP supervision. Most of the code in the project doesn't need to know about the details that make it so robust, though. That's the magic of good layered design.

In the next chapter, we'll take a look at some ways to customize your Nerves projects.

3.　https://github.com/groxio-learning/veml6030

CHAPTER 7

React to Change

A funny thing happened on the way to finishing this book. Covid hit the global electronic supply chain especially hard. Our reviewers and beta testers were reporting that they couldn't get hardware. As that happened, we had to find a way to solve the supply chain problems and update our code to use the new hardware.

Frank put his circuit board design skills into motion to build a custom-printed circuit board (PCB), complete with LEDs, the SPI interface, and the Raspberry Pi interface our board needed. He also pulled together a notebook in LiveBook, an evolving technology for experimenting with Elixir projects, including Nerves. Notebooks are documents holding both prose and code.

As we played with the new system, we made several tweaks to the binary clock. Instead of using an AM/PM indicator, we decided to use a 24-hour clock instead. We decided to change up the binary representation, for fun (more on that later). We also had to tweak the underlying SPI interface to work with the new system. To make these changes, we had to test the very techniques we put into place to build the clock in the first place. The supply chain upheaval gave us an excellent opportunity to take our own advice.

In this chapter, we'll walk you through how the new hardware works. We'll experiment with the project using a notebook that implements a prototype using Elixir to power our one-board binary clock. We'll change up a few of the details, like the AM/PM indicator and the way we represent time with bits.

Fair warning—we're not going to do all of the work for you this time around. Once we have a working prototype in a notebook, we'll let you build out the clock yourself so you can explore the concepts in this book in the context of a full Nerves project of your own.

We'll lay a foundation for you in the form of a prototype. Then it's your turn. You'll use the ideas in that notebook to build out a project using the techniques from this book. When you're done, you'll have your own binary clock. Let's get started.

Order a Custom Binary Clock Chip

To control supply chain problems, we took steps beyond the reach of the typical electronics hobbyist. Frank designed a single PCB with all of the LEDs, Raspberry Pi interfaces, and a constant current driver in one small package. While we were at it, we shifted the overall look of the binary clock to provide an interesting twist on our original problem.

Here's how we'll present the second iteration of the binary clock. This clock will work on binary representations of decimal digits. That means the largest possible time is 23:59:59. We'll need six digits to represent that time. The ones digits will need four bits each, and the tens digits will need two bits for the hours and three bits for each of the minutes and seconds, like this:

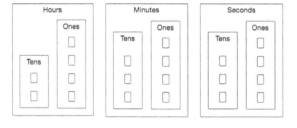

Notice the hours component has two digits, and the previous figure has two columns. The first has the two ones digits. Two bits can represent numbers 0–3, and that's enough for the 23-hour maximum for our hours digits. The right column has the four bits making up the tens digit. Four bits can represent integers 0–15, so that's enough for our tens digit that could have values 0–9. The new clock design has two digits each for hours, minutes, and seconds.

The binary clock as a PCB will have LEDs on the board itself laid out in this pattern. To read the clock, you'll read each column as a separate digit and then put them together to make a time.

Build a Printed Circuit Board

Since we wanted to be able to build the binary clock with fewer supply chain issues, Frank looked into building a printed circuit board made entirely of more available components, but ones that worked well with the Raspberry Pi and Nerves. This strategy would give our users a better chance at finding hardware for the binary clock project. He looked at a vendor called JLCPCB and investigated their parts availability. Their custom-printed boards are amazingly inexpensive for building simple things. You can find a parts list[1] to see the list we chose from.

Look at the Datasheet

The constant current driver we used is called the TM1620. We couldn't read Chinese, but Nerves Core Team member Jon Carstens found an English translation of the original TM1620 datasheet. We decided to give it a try.

Titan Micro makes many LED drivers. The TM1620 is one of the simpler versions they make and it can drive 48 LEDs, more than the 18 we needed. The datasheet[2] has all of the information we need to operate the interface. Open up the English version of that PDF and scan through it. You'll find several different parts.

Generally, we're looking for two important pieces of information. The first is the flow we need for initializing the driver and lighting the LEDs. The second is the actual format the LEDs use.

In the first four sections, you'll find an overview describing the interface and three sections on pin definitions. Since our pins will connect directly to the Pi Zero, we'll skip over those. The next few sections walk you through the instructions we'll use to connect to the interface and transmit data as times. About halfway through the document you'll find a flow chart that walks through the interactions we'll need to program into our clock.

The circuit diagram in the datasheet showed LEDs hooked up in a grid pattern. SEGn wires are the rows. The GRIDn wires are columns. You can see how we hooked up the LEDs in the schematic in the GitHub directory.[3] Here's what

---

1.   https://jlcpcb.com/parts
2.   https://github.com/fhunleth/binary_clock/tree/main/datasheets
3.   https://github.com/fhunleth/binary_clock/blob/main/hw

the two hours digits look like. Notice the GRiD1 and GRiD2 labels. The horizontal labels, from bottom to top, are SEG1 through SEG4:

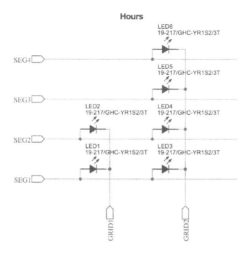

You can see the grid-style layout of the hours digit where each digit has rows and columns. The minutes and seconds are similar but use GRID3 through GRID6. Now that we know a little bit about the layout, we can start to play with them.

Configure Your Hardware

You can find the details for ordering the hardware at Frank's binary_clock GitHub project.[4] If you need a second Raspberry Pi Zero, you might want to order that too.

When you get your chip, plug it into the interface on your Pi. You'll plug in one micro-USB cable to the power port (the one closest to the end of the board) and a power source. Plug another cable to the micro-USB communications port. Eventually, the other end will plug into your computer, just as you did in earlier chapters.

Believe it or not, that's all of the assembly you need to do. This project will focus on the software aspects.

Load the LiveBook

Throughout this book, we've played with hardware by creating a new project using Mix and IEx because *we knew where we were going.* In this case, we have a new chip and we don't know quite how it works. It would be nice to

---

4.   https://github.com/fhunleth/binary_clock

start a pre-loaded project, plug in our Pi, and start to experiment right away. We'll also need to take notes as we go.

This is exactly the position Frank was in as he got his new hardware. He wanted to connect it, control it using Elixir, and then document his experience, all in one tool. As we were writing this book, the Nerves LiveBook project was ramping up.

Elixir's LiveBook combines the power of the Phoenix framework with an interactive *notebook*, a specialized file capable of handling Markdown prose, Elixir code, and output. Users can edit code or prose directly, and the LiveBook will take care of formatting the output and presenting the results to users. This combination works much like a scientist's lab and notebook, rolled into one. LiveBook authors can use it to present new tools to users, explore libraries, learn Elixir, or document the results of prototyping.

The Nerves version of LiveBook allows us to combine a working image with Circuits and a notebook so we can run code on an embedded system and add prose to document our experience as we go. We'll use this new tool to interact with our binary clock so we can experiment with the hardware without having to go through a long compilation cycle.

Since you already know how to burn firmware, getting started is going to be as easy as burning an image, inserting the card, and then plugging in the Pi.

Burn the Firmware

The Nerves LiveBook[5] project combines all of the power of Elixir's LiveBook[6] project with the build tools that make it so easy to build hardware projects with different targets. Part of the project is a series of builds already containing working installations of Elixir, Phoenix, LiveBook, and a few core Nerves libraries including Circuits.

Another part of the project is a codebase for building your own LiveBooks. Library and hardware vendors can use the project as a foundation and build their own series of firmwares for Nerves with LiveBook. We'll load prebuilt firmware from this repository and then copy a working LiveBook from another.

Go to the Nerves Livebook releases page.[7] Then click the Livebook firmware image for the Raspberry Pi Zero. The filename is nerves_livebook_rpi0.fw. Click the

---

5. https://github.com/livebook-dev/nerves_livebook
6. https://github.com/livebook-dev
7. https://github.com/livebook-dev/nerves_livebook/releases

link and download the file. Then, as you've done with other firmware projects, burn your firmware with fwup nerves_livebook_rpi0.fw from the directory that has your firmware.

Now you can plug in your Pi micro-USB cables. You'll see a heartbeat light for 50 seconds or so. When it turns solid, the LiveBook is ready. If it never blinks, always blinks, or goes dark, you have more troubleshooting to do. You'll find some troubleshooting instructions on the Nerves LiveBook GitHub page.

Import the Notebook

Now you should have a working bit of firmware running on your Pi. Phoenix is running. You can try it out by visiting your project on nerves.local.[8] The password is nerves. Type it in and you'll be redirected to the LiveBook home page. We'll use that page to load in the LiveBook for the binary clock.

When all is said and done, a LiveBook is a mixture of text and code. The text is in *Markdown* form, a user-friendly format for marking up text with things like headings, bullet lists, and the like. The code is in Elixir scripts. Running the LiveBook lets you experiment with the code by running it and even making tiny changes. That's the experience we're after.

As you work through the LiveBook in this chapter, we'll paste some of the snippets you will see into *this* book so you'll be able to tell what's happening as we describe the programs. If at any point you find the snippets are *different*, you should prefer the version of code in the *LiveBook* because that repository is easier to keep up to date and will show important changes before this book will.

The code we're going to be loading is in the fhunleth/binary_clock[9] project. Open the project in a new browser tab. We'll import the notebook as pure text. From the main directory in the GitHub project, click the file binary_clock.livemd. Then click the icon to copy the contents of the file to your clipboard.

Once you've copied the notebook to your clipboard, go back to the LiveBook homepage[10] on your Pi. Click the *Import* button next to the *New Notebook* button. Then click the *From clipboard* tab and paste the contents of your clipboard, and click the *Import* button to finalize the import as shown.

---

8.   http://nerves.local
9.   https://github.com/fhunleth/binary_clock
10.   http://nerves.local

When you're done, you'll see a notebook with all of the results of our research. What's more, rather than a single script, you can see several different snippets that initialize the binary clock, set up individual digits in the time, and light various LED patterns.

With a codified plan in the form of a notebook, we can shift gears. Let's look at the hardware for the new project. It will be much simpler this time around because we're having most of these concepts built into their own chip.

Bringing up the Binary Clock PCB the First Time

The Raspberry Pi is connected to the TM1620 on the custom binary clock board via the SPI bus. The first thing to do is to use Circuits.SPI to open the bus.

By far the trickiest part about the TM1620 is noticing that the bits are sent as little-endian. That means least significant bytes go first. The figure from section 8, figure 5, from the datasheet shows that B0, the least significant byte, goes first:

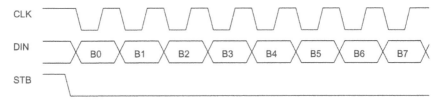

SPI normally sends data as big-endian. Luckily, Circuits.SPI has an lsb_first option to send data in exactly the format we need.

The second tricky part about the TM1620 is that the data bits (DIN) get sampled when the CLK line goes low to high. Once again, you can see this in action in section 8, figure 5, since the clock goes up in the middle of when each bit is on the wire. This is a SPI bus thing that's called mode. There are four SPI modes. Many Nerves SPI interfaces use mode 0, the default value for Circuit.SPI. The TM1620 uses SPI mode 3. The Circuit.SPI.open/2[11] docs describe modes in more detail.

With all of that information in mind, go to the first Elixir code cell in your notebook that has some code to open the SPI bus, like this:

```
alias Circuits.SPI

{:ok, spi} = SPI.open("spidev0.0", mode: 3, lsb_first: true)
```

---

11. https://hexdocs.pm/circuits_spi/Circuits.SPI.html#open/2

You can execute the code cell by simply clicking the Evaluate button just above the cell, on the left:

Once you click it, if all is working correctly, it will open the serial port interface between the Raspberry Pi and your binary clock PCB.

SPI Communication

The next step is to send data to the TM1620 to make it turn on an LED. The flow chart on page 7 of the datasheet shows how to do this:

1. Send the command to set the display mode.
2. Send the command to write to data memory.
3. Send the data bytes describing which LEDs to turn on and off.
4. Send the command to turn the LEDs on and set their brightness.

In short, we set the *display mode*, send a *write command*, send the *data* to write, and then send the command to *set brightness and go*. We'll take each one of those in turn.

Set the Display Mode

To follow the instructions on the datasheet to set the mode, we need to send 0b00000010, or just the number 2. Click evaluate on the notebook's Elixir cell that has this code:

```
SPI.transfer(spi, <<0b00000010>>)
```

The code sends a SPI command to transfer a binary 10, or a 2. We're off to the races.

Send the Write Command

The mode is set, so we can send the *write* command. The flow chart says to send 0x40 to write, so we'll do so. Click the evaluate button for this code:

```
SPI.transfer(spi, <<0x40>>)
```

Just as before, we transfer one value, a Hex 40. We're ready for the next step.

Send the Data

Next is to send the command to store bytes at address 0 and then the LED state. The flowchart says the command to do this is 0xc0, followed by the data. Remember, our data is laid out in a 6x8 grid.

There's a simpler way to think about our data, though. Each of the six grid columns are digits, and each of the columns contains the bits for one of the digits. That means all we need to do is send each of the digits as two bytes. The first byte is the digit, and the second is zero.

For example, if we want the binary clock to show the time 12:34:56, we'd send the digits 1, 2, 3, 4, 5, 6 in binary using this Elixir binary:

```
SPI.transfer(spi, <<0xC0, 1, 0, 2, 0, 3, 0, 4, 0, 5, 0, 6, 0>>)
```

The first digit is the command 0xC0 to write the data. The next two bytes are the tens digit of the hour 12, followed by a zero. Next, you have 2, 0 for the hours ones digits, the 3, 0 for the minutes tens digits, and so on. We've sent the time, and we're ready to light it up.

Send the Brightness

The final step is to send the command to turn the TM1620 on and set the brightness. This is shown in the table at the bottom of page 3. The dimmest value is 0x88. The brightest value is 0x8f. 0x80 is off. We'll use an intermediate brightness of 0x88, like this:

```
SPI.transfer(spi, <<0x88>>)
```

Let there be lights! Hopefully it shows what you'd expect. If you want to change it, modify the 0xc0 command above.

Our code works, but we can do a little better. We can roll these concepts up into a simple prototype that describes our clock.

Simple Clock

Now we have some building blocks to work with. We know the hardware works and that we can open the clock via the SPI. We can also set individual bit patterns representing time. We can use those blocks to piece together a basic clock prototype.

We'll start with a short module for setting the time. For now, we'll assume the SPI is already open and that we have access to it via a spi reference. We'll create two functions in the module. One will turn all of the LEDs off. The other will set a time given an open spi reference along with integer values representing hours, minutes, seconds, and brightness for the time display.

Show the Time

Let's start with the show function:

```
defmodule Clock do
  def show(spi, hours, minutes, seconds, brightness \\ 0) do
    with {:ok, _} <- SPI.transfer(spi, <<0x02>>),
         {:ok, _} <- SPI.transfer(spi, <<0x40>>),
         {:ok, _} <- SPI.transfer(spi,
           [0xC0, to_bcd(hours), to_bcd(minutes), to_bcd(seconds)]),
         {:ok, _} <- SPI.transfer(spi, <<0x88 + brightness>>) do
      :ok
    end
  end
```

We define the module and then open a show function, specifying the spi. We add integer values for hours, minutes, seconds, and a brightness ranging from 0..15 with a default of 0.

Next, we use Elixir's with statement to execute statements, as long as each statement successfully matches a tagged two-tuple beginning with :ok. We do all four of the steps in the flowchart, sending a 0x02 to set the display mode, a 0x40 to write to memory. a 0xc plus data to send the time, and a brightness to trigger the transfer at the specified brightness. We're ready to move on.

Turn the LEDs Off

Next, we can define the off function:

```
def off(spi) do
  SPI.transfer(spi, <<0x80>>)
end
```

We simply transfer a 0x00 to the SPI interface, turning all of the LEDs off. That's all we need to do. Next, we build helper functions to represent digits.

Translate Numerals to Binaries with Digits

The final step in our clock prototype is to build the individual digit clusters for hours, minutes, and seconds:

```
  def to_bcd(value) when value >= 0 and value < 100 do
    <<div(value, 10), 0, rem(value, 10), 0>>
  end
end
```

The function head takes a single value from 0..99. We add some guards to validate the values. Then, we build a binary with the tens digit, a zero, and the ones digit. That's all we need for this simple Clock prototype. As long as we give it a valid open SPI interface and a working time, the functions will work.

You can test drive it. Find the notebook cell defining the Clock module. You'll see a line of the code at the bottom that looks like this:

```
Clock.show(spi, 12, 34, 56)
```

In the notebook, click the evaluate button for that cell. When you send those values, you'll see the clock light up with the binary digit patterns for 1, 2, 3, 4, 5, and 6. You're adding layers to your initial prototype!

Build an Animation

To build something a bit more exciting, you can use the LiveBook component library called Kino. It has an animation service. To get a sense for what the clock will look like in motion, enter this code. It starts at a random time and runs way faster than real time to be more exciting:

```
starting_time = :rand.uniform(86400)

Kino.animate(50, starting_time, fn seconds ->
  h = seconds |> div(3600)
  m = seconds |> div(60) |> rem(60)
  s = seconds |> rem(60)

  md = Kino.Markdown.new("Clock: `#{h}:#{m}:#{s}`")

  Clock.show(spi, h, m, s)

  {:cont, md, seconds + 1}
end)
```

This code calls the same code repeatedly, rendering md repeatedly and setting the new state to seconds + 1. Marvel at your animated clock.

Now we have a pretty good idea how the clock works. We know enough to build a proper mix project. The next step is to branch your code in your source control system (or just copy it if you're not using source control) and make just enough changes to make the project work with the new clock.

Now we'll hand the project over to you to complete. You can decide how you want to finish your clock. We'll give you a few ideas in the following section.

What You'll Build

This chapter walks through the process of building a LiveBook notebook to work with hardware. The notebook serves as a documented prototype of sorts. It has the basics of interacting with our new custom PCB.

To get LiveBook running, we burned pre-built firmware, connected the Pi to the host, started the device, and then connected to the internet over nerves.local. Then we loaded a notebook that describes how to use the new binary clock. The notebook describes in both code and prose the process of starting the clock and pushing a time to it, step by step.

When we were done, we could push individual times to the clock and even run an animation.

Why It Matters

Notebooks smooth out some of the inherent friction that comes with Nerves. By working with pre-defined firmware and notebooks, you can experiment by sending tiny commands to your hardware and then document your experiences. Nerves and LiveBook take care of the rest.

With a notebook in hand, you have a tiny documented prototype. Now you can use it as a foundation of a new binary clock. Only this time, you get to build it yourself.

Try It Yourself

This *easy* problem deals with making a binary clock in the notebook.

Make a single binary Clock module work from the notebook using a Kino animation. You'll need to make three changes to do so.

- Add an open/0 function to open the clock. Use this function to open the SPI interface and return a spi reference.

- Build a start/0 function to start the Kino animation with one-second intervals.

- Replace the starting_time with the current time.

This *medium* problem moves the notebook research into a Mix project.

Make a new Git project, or fork your existing one, to use the PCB binary clock instead of the one we built by hand in the previous chapters. To do so, you'll need to make a few changes.

- You'll need to change the functional core to have the right datatype and specify the right values for test, development, and production modes. You may decide to rewrite the core from scratch.

- You'll need to change the code that opens the PCB through Circuits.SPI using the code from the notebook.

- You'll need to change the code that sends data to the PCB using the notebook prototype as a model.

- You may need to tweak other code to make this work.

This *hard* problem is like the *medium* problem but supports both versions of the binary clock from the same software platform.

- Modify your existing binary clock built from the previous chapters with a new program.

What's Next?

You've used Elixir, Nerves, and a few hardware components to build a binary clock two different ways. You don't need to stop here. If you find these problems interesting, you can build your own digital clock and even build in alarm clocks or timers.

The great thing about working with Nerves is that for large stretches of time you can forget you're working with hardware altogether. We expect you to work with more hardware. Even if your hobbies and career take you down another path, we hope you'll find techniques in this book that will set you up for success. Building layered applications that compose well is the best way to break down complex problems into tiny pieces that work together.

Wherever this journey takes you, we want to hear from you. If you build some version of a binary clock, we'd love to see it. We're interested in your hardware, the cases you put them in, and the software you use to power them. Enjoy the road!

Bibliography

[IT19]   James Edward Gray, II and Bruce A. Tate. *Designing Elixir Systems with OTP*. The Pragmatic Bookshelf, Raleigh, NC, 2019.

[Tho18]   Dave Thomas. *Programming Elixir 1.6*. The Pragmatic Bookshelf, Raleigh, NC, 2018.

Thank you!

We hope you enjoyed this book and that you're already thinking about what you want to learn next. To help make that decision easier, we're offering you this gift.

Head over to https://pragprog.com right now and use the coupon code BUYAN-OTHER2021 to save 30% on your next ebook. Void where prohibited or restricted. This offer does not apply to any edition of the *The Pragmatic Programmer* ebook.

And if you'd like to share your own expertise with the world, why not propose a writing idea to us? After all, many of our best authors started off as our readers, just like you. With a 50% royalty, world-class editorial services, and a name you trust, there's nothing to lose. Visit https://pragprog.com/become-an-author/ today to learn more and to get started.

We thank you for your continued support, and we hope to hear from you again soon!

The Pragmatic Bookshelf

Pragmatic Bookshelf

SAVE 30%!
Use coupon code
BUYANOTHER2022

Build a Weather Station with Elixir and Nerves

The Elixir programming language has become a go-to tool for creating reliable, fault-tolerant, and robust server-side applications. Thanks to Nerves, those same exact benefits can be realized in embedded applications. This book will teach you how to structure, build, and deploy production grade Nerves applications to network-enabled devices. The weather station sensor hub project that you will be embarking upon will show you how to create a full stack IoT solution in record time. You will build everything from the embedded Nerves device to the Phoenix backend and even the Grafana time-series data visualizations.

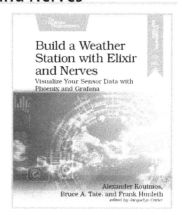

Alexander Koutmos, Bruce A. Tate, Frank Hunleth
(90 pages) ISBN: 9781680509021. $26.95
https://pragprog.com/book/passweather

Designing Elixir Systems with OTP

You know how to code in Elixir; now learn to think in it. Learn to design libraries with intelligent layers that shape the right data structures, flow from one function into the next, and present the right APIs. Embrace the same OTP that's kept our telephone systems reliable and fast for over 30 years. Move beyond understanding the OTP functions to knowing what's happening under the hood, and why that matters. Using that knowledge, instinctively know how to design systems that deliver fast and resilient services to your users, all with an Elixir focus.

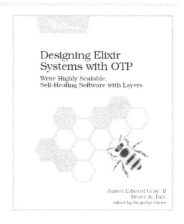

James Edward Gray, II and Bruce A. Tate
(246 pages) ISBN: 9781680506617. $41.95
https://pragprog.com/book/jgotp

Programming Elixir 1.6

This book is *the* introduction to Elixir for experienced programmers, completely updated for Elixir 1.6 and beyond. Explore functional programming without the academic overtones (tell me about monads just one more time). Create concurrent applications, but get them right without all the locking and consistency headaches. Meet Elixir, a modern, functional, concurrent language built on the rock-solid Erlang VM. Elixir's pragmatic syntax and built-in support for metaprogramming will make you productive and keep you interested for the long haul. Maybe the time is right for the Next Big Thing. Maybe it's Elixir.

Dave Thomas
(410 pages) ISBN: 9781680502992. $47.95
https://pragprog.com/book/elixir16

Programming Ecto

Languages may come and go, but the relational database endures. Learn how to use Ecto, the premier database library for Elixir, to connect your Elixir and Phoenix apps to databases. Get a firm handle on Ecto fundamentals with a module-by-module tour of the critical parts of Ecto. Then move on to more advanced topics and advice on best practices with a series of recipes that provide clear, step-by-step instructions on scenarios commonly encountered by app developers. Co-authored by the creator of Ecto, this title provides all the essentials you need to use Ecto effectively.

Darin Wilson and Eric Meadows-Jönsson
(242 pages) ISBN: 9781680502824. $45.95
https://pragprog.com/book/wmecto

Programming Phoenix 1.4

Don't accept the compromise between fast and beautiful: you can have it all. Phoenix creator Chris McCord, Elixir creator José Valim, and award-winning author Bruce Tate walk you through building an application that's fast and reliable. At every step, you'll learn from the Phoenix creators not just what to do, but why. Packed with insider insights and completely updated for Phoenix 1.4, this definitive guide will be your constant companion in your journey from Phoenix novice to expert as you build the next generation of web applications.

Chris McCord, Bruce Tate and José Valim
(356 pages) ISBN: 9781680502268. $45.95
https://pragprog.com/book/phoenix14

Metaprogramming Elixir

Write code that writes code with Elixir macros. Macros make metaprogramming possible and define the language itself. In this book, you'll learn how to use macros to extend the language with fast, maintainable code and share functionality in ways you never thought possible. You'll discover how to extend Elixir with your own first-class features, optimize performance, and create domain-specific languages.

Chris McCord
(128 pages) ISBN: 9781680500417. $17
https://pragprog.com/book/cmelixir

Mastering Clojure Macros

Level up your skills by taking advantage of Clojure's powerful macro system. Macros make hard things possible and normal things easy. They can be tricky to use, and this book will help you deftly navigate the terrain. You'll discover how to write straightforward code that avoids duplication and clarifies your intentions. You'll learn how and why to write macros. You'll learn to recognize situations when using a macro would (and wouldn't!) be helpful. And you'll use macros to remove unnecessary code and build new language features.

Colin Jones
(120 pages) ISBN: 9781941222225. $17
https://pragprog.com/book/cjclojure

Functional Programming Patterns in Scala and Clojure

Solve real-life programming problems with a fraction of the code that pure object-oriented programming requires. Use Scala and Clojure to solve in-depth problems and see how familiar object-oriented patterns can become more concise with functional programming and patterns. Your code will be more declarative, with fewer bugs and lower maintenance costs.

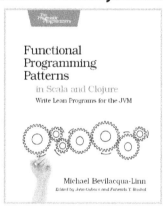

Michael Bevilacqua-Linn
(256 pages) ISBN: 9781937785475. $36
https://pragprog.com/book/mbfpp

The Pragmatic Bookshelf

The Pragmatic Bookshelf features books written by professional developers for professional developers. The titles continue the well-known Pragmatic Programmer style and continue to garner awards and rave reviews. As development gets more and more difficult, the Pragmatic Programmers will be there with more titles and products to help you stay on top of your game.

Visit Us Online

This Book's Home Page
https://pragprog.com/book/thnerves
Source code from this book, errata, and other resources. Come give us feedback, too!

Keep Up to Date
https://pragprog.com
Join our announcement mailing list (low volume) or follow us on twitter @pragprog for new titles, sales, coupons, hot tips, and more.

New and Noteworthy
https://pragprog.com/news
Check out the latest pragmatic developments, new titles and other offerings.

Save on the ebook

Save on the ebook versions of this title. Owning the paper version of this book entitles you to purchase the electronic versions at a terrific discount.

PDFs are great for carrying around on your laptop—they are hyperlinked, have color, and are fully searchable. Most titles are also available for the iPhone and iPod touch, Amazon Kindle, and other popular e-book readers.

Send a copy of your receipt to support@pragprog.com and we'll provide you with a discount coupon.

Contact Us

Online Orders: *https://pragprog.com/catalog*
Customer Service: *support@pragprog.com*
International Rights: *translations@pragprog.com*
Academic Use: *academic@pragprog.com*
Write for Us: *http://write-for-us.pragprog.com*
Or Call: +1 800-699-7764

Lightning Source UK Ltd.
Milton Keynes UK
UKHW030935220822
407646UK00005B/15